THE
HOLLYWOOD
H·A·N·D·B·O·O·K

ROBIN GREER
and
SARAH REINHARDT
with
KEVIN DORNAN

DOVE
BOOKS

ISBN 0-7871-1174-0

Printed in the United States of America

Dove Books
8955 Beverly Boulevard
West Hollywood, CA 90048
(310) 786-1600

Join Dove on the World Wide Web at: www.doveaudio.com/dove/

Distributed by Penguin USA

Text design and layout by Folio Graphics
Cover design by Rick Penn-Kraus
Cover and interior photography by Ann Bogart

First Printing: May 1997

10   9   8   7   6   5   4   3   2   1

THE
HOLLYWOOD
H·A·N·D·B·O·O·K

Dedication

Sarah's family—for loving and believing in me so much as to drive me out of town

Lynn Geller—thanks for the automatic yesses and nos, and her all-around hilarity through the years

Robin's family—for loving and supporting me, even though they still have no clue as to what I do

Kevin thanks Mother Theresa and the little people

CONTENTS

THE
HOLLYWOOD
H·A·N·D·B·O·O·K

INTRODUCTION

Hollywood, California: It's not a place, it's a state of mind. Because in this city, you can be anything you want just because you believe you are. You, too, can be a rock star. All you have to do is dress like one and take the right drugs; you don't even have to play an instrument. Isn't that great?! Hollywood is a place where you can rent an apartment, lease a flashy car, print up some phony business cards, and voilà! You're a producer! You can call yourself a model, even if the only ramp you walk is a stretch of pavement near Sunset and Vine. Wanna be a celebrity? Just give the right actor oral gratification in his rental car, and the next thing you know, you're more "divinely" famous than he is. That's right, it can happen to you, and it can only happen here.

Does this sound like the kind of lifestyle you could pretend to have? Then you have just purchased your new bible. If you follow all of the suggestions within these wise and witty pages, then this way of life can soon be yours.

In *The Hollywood Handbook*, we explain it all to you: how to be anything you want to be or, at the very least, fool others into thinking that's what you are. It's so easy, so simple, and it's all right here in front of you.

This book is the key that unlocks the door to . . . to . . . MECCA!

So, readers, read on. Your life is about to change. Throw away whatever stability you have or pretend to have. You don't need it anymore. You're a dreamer now. If you were here, we'd give you a big hug. You're about to become one of us, and there's no turning back. Why would you want to? That life was suppressing you, holding you back from being the true you. The you we know you are. So get ready! You've got places to go, people to see, deals to make, bars to crawl. Let's go!

HOLLYWOOD WANNA-BE

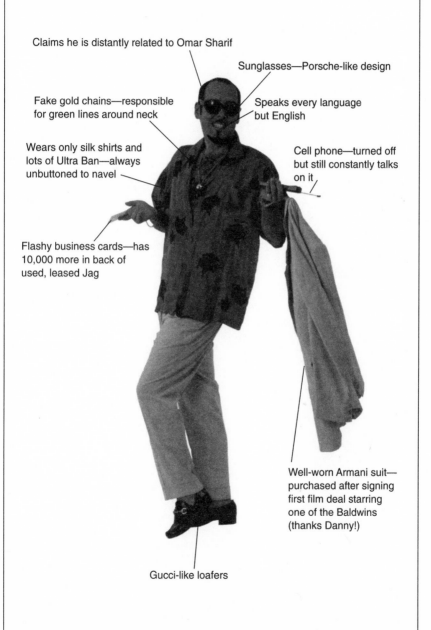

Claims he is distantly related to Omar Sharif

Sunglasses—Porsche-like design

Fake gold chains—responsible for green lines around neck

Speaks every language but English

Wears only silk shirts and lots of Ultra Ban—always unbuttoned to navel

Cell phone—turned off but still constantly talks on it

Flashy business cards—has 10,000 more in back of used, leased Jag

Well-worn Armani suit—purchased after signing first film deal starring one of the Baldwins (thanks Danny!)

Gucci-like loafers

GETTING STARTED

W hatever means of transport brought you here to this holy land, it's time to get started on your journey through, around, and over this place we call the "City of Angels" (and we're not talking one of Raphael's models). You're here! You need a place to base. This could mean a lot of things. It could mean sleeping on a couch at a friend's from college who's a PA (production assistant/slave) at Warner Bros. (whose only job requirement was a working car). Or, slowly chipping away at that nest egg at a motel on Western Ave. somewhere between Hollywood Blvd. and Olympic. Or, possibly, for the select few, moving into that mansion hideaway in Beverly Hills where the only requirements for staying there are sex, drugs, and

an ability to turn a blind eye to the age difference of your landlord/lover/bank account. By the way, you don't have to be sporting the female anatomy for this; all genders may apply.

In any event, you've made it here somehow, and you're living here somewhere. Consult our trusty map on pages 34–35 to see if you're living in the right place. If not, make it up. Join the crowd. After all, *an ounce of reinvention makes a pound of pretention.*

Here's a good first-week starter list:

1. Start drinking lots of coffee.

2. Hair: if not blond or chic and greasy, change.

3. Try not to overdo that fashion statement you loved back home. Blending in helps. Keep it simple and don't make waves.

4. Your first purchase should be a car, since you'll be driving everywhere—including to your kitchen. Don't *ever* be caught walking (major huge faux pas).

5. Food: Restaurants are out—huge giant major faux pas to be seen at a place that has lost its culinary cache, so better to do the drive-thru thing than ruin your reputation before you've even gotten one.

6. Tanning salon: for that necessary California "I'm healthier than you are" glow. No reason to waste a week at the beach when you can sizzle for just 16 minutes and $12.

7. On the seventh day, hit Thrifty Drugs and buy that full-length mirror. Pick the one that makes you look fatter than you are—it keeps you on point. Unless you're as funny as Roseanne, *fat doesn't work*, so put down those Reese's Pieces and crunch, crunch, crunch.

By the way, if you haven't yet realized the importance of being daily, as in *Variety* and *The Hollywood Reporter*, not to mention joining a gym, then you might as well see if that job at Long John Silver's at Wal-Mart Plaza back home is still available.

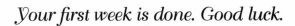

Your first week is done. Good luck.

TRENDS

Keep in mind that trends are transitory and subject to change. For example, in the early 1980s, leg warmers and cropped sweatshirts (à la *Flashdance*) were all the rage. If you wore that today, you'd be laughed out of the gym. In the late 1980s, it was appropriate to wear a tight black dress and stilettos to breakfast. We don't do this in the 1990s because we don't have sex in the 1990s, so why taunt? In any event, you understand what we're saying. Trends can change in a fleeting moment, so as important as the information in this chapter is, by the time you're reading it, it will probably be obsolete. Still, we will do what we can to steer you away from your inevitable out-of-date attire and attitude.

Choose wisely and choose well.

TRENDY ACCESSORIES

Body Piercing was once considered part of a tribal ritual. But now, at least in Hollywood, it's just one more thing to do to freak out your friends and family. Won't Mom get a big kick out of that huge silver crucifix punched into your tongue?

Tattoos can be a colorful and individual statement, but remember, they're like marriage, only more permanent.

Baseball Caps (The New Toupee) can say so much about you—depending on whether you wear it forward or backward.

Cellular Phones and Beepers are the modern-day electronic accessories that used to be reserved for rich Arabs and drug dealers. Now, even if you can't pay your rent, both items are affordable. In fact, LA Cellular has a curbside employee standing by when you arrive at LAX.

Anklets and Belly Chains are usually reserved for summer, but they can be worn at any time, and that's where body piercing comes in handy. Your belly chain can start at your nostrils if you feel like it; the possibilities are limitless.

Handbags As of this writing, Prada is the moneybag of the moment.

Nail Color is a "What's new today?" thing; you should ask your manicurist weekly what color to wear. Black today, green tomorrow—every week it's a new color, and there's nothing worse than being caught wearing last week's purple when everyone else in town has already moved on to today's yellow frost.

Sunglasses should be determined by whatever your favorite star is wearing in his/her latest movie.

Hair Extensions were an eighties thing but are now making a comeback. We know they can be a bit awkward on a first date, but hopefully he won't get his fingers caught. Hey—what are you doing making out on a first date, anyway?

Bottled Water can be any brand, but Evian seems to be most favored by the traveling elite.

Scripts are the best thing to read while doing anything—working the Stairmaster at the gym, waiting in a coffee shop, etc. They make you look important and are a good icebreaker for any conversation.

The Latest Fiction is not what you are secretly reading under your night-light, it's what people should *think* you are reading. It's what you should carry around with you with your script during the day. Stick with the "hip beyond hip" authors. These can be found at your more artsy bookstores, such as Book Soup, Midnight Special, and Illiterature, to name a few. As for the always hip authors, some safe bets are Thomas Pynchon, James Ellroy, Kurt Vonnegut, Vladimir Nabokov, Charles Bukowski, William Burroughs, and

John Fowles. If you really want to appeal to the intellectual artsy crowd, pick up Nietzsche.

Magazines are important because they help you keep up with all the new trends and current gossip. Don't worry about being seen reading the tabloids—everyone does it.

Dogs are separated into guy dogs and girl dogs, even though some cross over, depending on where you live. On the Westside, they tend not to cross over unless you're stuck with it in the break-up or divorce. Guy dogs are generally named Buddy or Joe, or some "I am hetero and this is my pal" name. They tend to be Labradors, German Shepherds, pit bulls, or any other mid-to-large-sized dog that looks good in the back of a Jeep. Girl dogs are anything cute or pretty: Malteses, Yorkshire terriers, bichons frises, Samoyeds, white Akitas with blue eyes, or any dog that will complement your image. Like scripts, dogs are good conversation openers.

Children can be a problem, because when they go out of style, they'll be too spoiled and pretentious for anyone else to adopt. Luckily, that's why boarding schools were invented.

WESTSIDE TRENDY GIRL

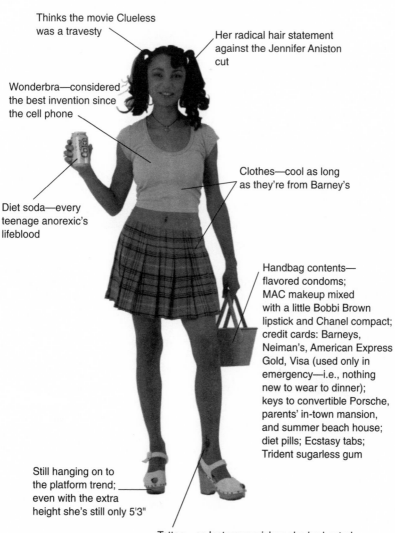

Thinks the movie Clueless was a travesty

Her radical hair statement against the Jennifer Aniston cut

Wonderbra—considered the best invention since the cell phone

Clothes—cool as long as they're from Barney's

Diet soda—every teenage anorexic's lifeblood

Handbag contents—flavored condoms; MAC makeup mixed with a little Bobbi Brown lipstick and Chanel compact; credit cards: Barneys, Neiman's, American Express Gold, Visa (used only in emergency—i.e., nothing new to wear to dinner); keys to convertible Porsche, parents' in-town mansion, and summer beach house; diet pills; Ecstasy tabs; Trident sugarless gum

Still hanging on to the platform trend; even with the extra height she's still only 5'3"

Tattoo—so last year; wishes she had opted for an anklet—much easier to remove; considers it a "life lesson"

TRENDY DISEASES

If you really want to fit in, you must develop one of the following afflictions, or else you'll have nothing to talk about with your new friends. This move is necessary to make sure the focus stays on you. Preferably, you'll choose a disease that won't cause you too much damage.

Chronic Fatigue Syndrome or Epstein-Barr is easy to maintain because even though most people in the health profession will argue its very existence, you can convince everyone else you have it by sleeping a lot.

Alcoholism and Drug Addiction are always sure bets. You don't even have to have the disease; just use your imagination to make up great "war stories" (an AA and NA term for life before sobriety) and you'll fit right in.

Chlamydia can be helpful—it takes the pressure off that first date, and if you're asked out again, you will know they love you for you.

Bulimia and Anorexia are always popular, and either makes keeping up with the latest fashion trends a snap. You'll have no trouble getting into those A-line skirts and size 1 jeans. Nothing like killing two birds with one stone!

Gambling is great—it means frequent trips to Vegas. Everyone of any importance has his or her own bookie.

Overeating is okay only if you want to be an agent or producer, because those are the only professions in which it's not necessary to be attractive to get laid.

Sex and Love Addiction are okay; in fact, 90 percent of the people in town have it, but it's sex and love with *themselves,* even when they're with you.

Tourette's Syndrome comes in handy because you can curse at everyone and get away with it.

ADD (Attention Deficit Disorder) is a good excuse for being fickle. Julia Roberts obviously suffers from it, since she can't stay with one boyfriend or husband for more than 15 minutes. It's the perfect disease if you're easily bored.

Aixelsyd (Dyslexia) is easy; if the first spelling of this looked right to you, then you clearly have it.

Heart Murmurs will get you no sympathy, since no one in Hollywood has a heart and no one will care if yours is murmuring.

Obsessive-Compulsive Disorder allows you many excuses. If you're chronically late, it's because you had to run back into your house several times to rewash your hands and check the stove. We both have it, and it is our personal favorite. "Fashionably late" has taken on new meaning.

TRENDY PARTY TALK

You'll make a more interesting invite if you stay somewhat up to date on current events. We are not referring to what you might read in *The New York Times*, more like what you'd pick up in *Vanity Fair* or the *National Enquirer*. It's important to remember that when you take a stand, you must stick by that stand. For instance, if you've always thought Don was the best for Melanie, then you can't just switch to Antonio at the drop of a hat. You've got to stick with Don, no matter how unfashionable it might seem. Ultimately, you will be respected for holding your ground. Here are a few light and timely topics to bandy about at any social gathering or dinner party:

spirituality vs. materialism

Quentin Tarantino directing vs. Quentin Tarantino acting

astrology vs. numerology

high colonics vs. coffee enemas

Aspen vs. Sun Valley

spinning vs. Karate vs. Yoga

Range Rovers vs. Hummers

AIDS vs. breast cancer

Curtis School vs. John Thomas Dye School

money vs. fame

Anastasia facials vs. Vera facials

tabloids v. fashion mags

Brentwood vs. Beverly Hills

Umberto Salon vs. Deluxe Salon

Special K vs. Ecstasy

MISCELLANEOUS TRENDS

White Liberals Adopting Minority Babies This is mainly a celebrity trend (their way of justifying getting millions of dollars for nothing and making a social statement at the same time). However, the trickle-down theory seems to apply here: It's making its way around those in White America who have incomes over $100,000. Perhaps it's their way of alleviating the guilt for the turning back of affirmative action.

Eclectic Movies Although mostly slept through, it's a way of looking well-rounded and artsy.

Travel to Indigent Countries It ceased for a while after *Midnight Express* but picked up again after *The Sheltering Sky*. These days it seems that everyone has an over-stuffed album filled with shots from their African photo-safari.

Silver Patio Furniture seems to be a requirement for every rich bachelor/wanna-be producer in town. Constantly running out of stock in West Hollywood.

Conspiracy Theories used to be attributed to activists and protestors; thanks to Oliver Stone, they're now a common topic of conversation in just about every circle.

Terrorism Not too popular in social circles unless you're planning on joining a paramilitary group.

Vintage Cars Oh, so pricey but oh-so-cool.

Robert Frank *The Americans* is a must-have on any chic coffee table.

Scones Thanks to Merchant/Ivory and Emma Thompson films, scones are a way of showing your refinement and gentility. Make sure you order them with cream, not peanut butter.

Auctioning Stuff Dead People Used to Own Big money in this one. If Grandpa's famous enough, an old roll of unused toilet paper (stamped and framed) can pull in fifty grand.

American Spirit Cigarettes If you want to look like you have an edge but really don't know how to smoke. No need to inhale. In fact, you're better off that way.

Cigars #1 Hollywood rule: If Jack does it, it's cool.

Crossword Puzzles Start off with the *TV Guide*, then build to the *Los Angeles Times*, and finally the ultimate: *The New York Times*. Now you can go public—sit in any coffeehouse doing the puzzle while sipping a latte.

Whitening Toothpaste began with Topol for those who couldn't afford bleach or caps; now there are many to choose from. You'll never have to see a dentist again to mask those unwanted coffee and cigarette stains.

Aveda Anything Looks good and impressive around the bathtub. Proves you don't buy your shampoo at Thrifty.

Dennis Rodman and Brightly Colored Hair Dennis Rodman is so popular in L.A. that people think he plays for the Lakers; after all, he looks like he belongs here with his dresses, makeup, and brightly colored hair. He could be anyone walking down Santa Monica Blvd. in West Hollywood. He'll figure it out.

Flavored Vodka So much easier than mixers—it's the nineties' version of Seabreezes.

Hollywood Exposés Everyone is writing them; there are books about people who have dated stand-ins, stunt-men, extras, and PA's. The list goes on. People just want the inside on *anything* Hollywood.

Protests The front of the VA building is beginning to look like a seven-day-a-week block party.

Environmentally Friendly Anything Nowadays just about anything is recyclable—how about the renewed popularity of the Village People?

Las Vegas The only people who haven't figured out how popular LV is are the airlines. Unless you book a flight weeks in advance, either you can't get one or you might as well fly to Rio for the same price.

Two Bunch Palms Ever since the movie *The Player*, you must say the only reason you're feeling refreshed is because of that mud bath you had over the weekend.

Curfew Laws From any minor to major disturbance, from a riot to an earthquake to a loud stereo, those good ol' boys on Capitol Hill stand by with their wristwatches, waiting to put the youth of today to bed. The future is so much easier to deal with when it's safely tucked away sleeping.

Lesbianism Oh so trendy. If you can't be gay, at least be bi.

Tantra Sex Any excuse to try for a multiple orgasm.

Dalai Lama Oh, the metaphysical—so pretentious, yet so now.

Being Online An agoraphobe's dream come true. Soon there will be a major segment of the population suffering from atrophied bodies and huge muscular fingers who have lots of friends they've never met, not to mention closets full of useless junk ordered on the Internet.

10 WAYS TO TERRIFY A HOLLYWOOD HOUSEWIFE

Tell her:

1 Her husband's on his way home.

2 The maids have quit and she might have to make dinner.

3 The nanny has quit and she might have to take care of the children (or at least remember them).

4 Her charge card was declined at Barneys.

5 She unintentionally insulted Barbara Davis.

6 Her hairdresser got free tickets to Puerto Vallarta the weekend of the Academy Awards ceremony.

7 Her husband wants sex (with her).

8 There's an incredible sale at Gucci when she has the flu.

9 The FDA announced collagen is linked to Alzheimer's.

10 Her child punched one of Steven Spielberg's kids at preschool, and now her kid will never get into John Thomas Dye.

PLACES TO GO

PLACES TO MEET

PLACES TO MEET THE ELITE

If you're looking to meet men and women with real power, go to New York, Washington, or Tokyo. If you want to meet men and women who appear to have real power, here's a list of places where you should begin to look.

Monday ❀ Morton's owns this night. Anyone of any influence can be found here, chomping their meat and potatoes and pontificating while looking around the room to see who might be sitting in a better position, and then plotting how they will overthrow them by the following Monday.

Tuesday ❋ This is "impress a new client" night. There are a couple of options. The Ivy on Robertson, with its low-key lighting and soothing sounds of Billie Holiday wafting through the air, provides the perfect ambiance to romance a client over corn chowder and crab cakes. Also good on this night is Orso on 3rd Street—but only on the heated garden patio, where you will glimpse a splattering of celebrities. In Beverly Hills, a favorite of Arnold and Maria's and the filmmaking Scott brothers (Ridley and Tony, of course), among other Peking duck–savoring socialites, is Mr. Chow's.

Wednesday ❋ Drai's on La Cienega: With its gilded safari feel and its *Casablanca*-ish piano bar, graced by its very own Rick (Victor Drai himself), you, too, can feel like a movie star. No shortage of leggy starlets here. We think it's possible these women are one of two things: mistresses of men dining with their wives, or just ladies paid to sit and look good. In any case, it lends to the visual. By the way, the food is good, too. Another place to go is Eclipse, across from Morton's. This is a great place to entertain your larger group of out-of-town guests. They will be impressed with the ornate decor and recognize the owner, Bernard, from their last trip to town when you took them to Spago.

Thursday ❋ This is your party night. Everyone is unwinding from the week and revving up for the weekend. The Buffalo Club is the place to be, but first you have to make friends or sleep with one of the owners (from what we've heard, your better option is the former, otherwise plan on going there only once). This is your best shot at seeing Robert De Niro, Harvey Keitel, and Quentin Tarantino guffawing at one another at the same table. They won't acknowledge you, but you can tell all your friends you had dinner with them—after all, it's a small room. For a more low-key evening with the family, Toscana in Brentwood is nice: Good Italian food, and you will more than likely run into someone from the O.J. Simpson trial. (Not O.J. himself, though.

He is no longer permitted to dine north of Century Blvd.) On Beverly in West Hollywood, Le Colonial is the new hot spot. If you have a taste for Vietnamese and hope to catch a glimpse of Madonna, this is the place. It's hot, it's hip, it's now—for now.

Friday ❈ It's your last night to dine in town, since after dinner you'll be heading out to the beach house or, if you don't have one, hiding for the rest of the weekend. Why not have a nice Japanese meal at Matsuhisa on La Cienega. It's got the best sushi in town (it had better, since it's also got the longest wait). If your name isn't currently on a marquee, be there by the time the doors open for dinner, and maybe you'll be seated by nine. If you're already at the beach, go to 72 Market Street in Venice. You may see Angelica and Bob. Make sure you wear black, artsy jewelry—this is the chic Venice crowd. Also try Chinois on Main, another piece in Wolfgang Puck's restaurant Monopoly game. The Ivy at the Shore is Morton's Monday night crowd, only drunk.

Saturday ❈ Everyone's at their beach houses. There are really only about three restaurants at which you're allowed to be seen tonight. Granita is number one, but if you were wild in your younger days, beware: The decor triggers flashbacks. It's a great place to catch a glimpse of all your favorite celebrities and movie moguls in their jeans. Then there's Tradinoid. This is a family-run, quaint, and homey atmosphere. Always go with the special—Mama knows best.

Sunday ❈ It's safe to be seen in town again. For the old school, it's Matteo's in Westwood. You can see Ol' Blue Eyes staring blankly at the menu, looking for his entree namesake as you twist your spaghetti and meatballs, glancing at what's left of Old Hollywood. For more of the same, try Musso and Frank. For your younger crowd, there's Giorgio on Sunset. It's on your way home from the beach and perfectly positioned for your drive home to one of your destinations that will most likely be an offshoot of Sunset. This is also a good night to eat at home and refresh your memory of your children's names. It's always so embarrassing when you have to ask the maid.

WHERE THE HIP TRIP

Whether it's just to help you feel like you're part of what's happening, or to get laid by people who can't or won't support you, we have composed a partial list of places to go. Keep in mind these are all partial lists; after all, this is not a guidebook. (If you want that, go to your local bookstore and specifically ask for a guide-book.) Again, these are listed by the days of the week. Some of them are good any night, but we'll let you figure that out for yourselves.

Monday ❋ Bar Marmont, situated next to the ever-hip Chateau Marmont (remember John Belushi and Jim Morrison?) is one of those on-again/off-again places. It died for a while after Kato Kaelin made his grand appearance in 1995, but with their newly opened second bar, they are back in the swing of it. The Pearl is a quietly chic place to have drinks, and also conversation, if that's what you want. If conversation is not what you want, check out the Lava Lounge.

Tuesday ❋ Having first taken over the Olive crowd several years ago, then shut down after a fire, Jones is back. The Dresden Room is another good place, with its kitschy piano couple, Marty and Elaine, and open mike. You'll feel like you're in a David Lynch outtake. If you're on the Westside, Hal's on Abbot Kinney has a decent bar.

Wednesday ❋ The Derby in Los Feliz is the swinging place—lots of young kids who actually know how to dance without Ecstasy, and to music from a different era to boot. Also good if you're into a quiet, rubbernecking dinner is Pane Vino. A good bar and a great outside patio. If you're on the Eastside and want a drink, go to the Good Luck Bar.

Thursday ❋ The ever-grungy Three of Clubs is the place: dark and out of the way, but cheap drinks. On the Westside, check out Liquid Kitty, one of those places that will make you long for New York.

Friday ❋ The hard-to-believe-it's-still-standing Formosa Cafe is happening tonight—expect a lot of attitude from the ancient staff. Also good is Jack's Sugar Shack and the Sky Bar (at the Mondrian Hotel).

Saturday ❋ Get yourself invited to a party, or don't be seen anywhere.

Sunday ❋ Afternoon barbecues or recovery ("60 Minutes" and a book).

MISCELLANEOUS MUSIC PLACES

For all of the following, check the *LA Weekly* for listings.

The Viper Room, The Opium Den, Troubadour, McCabe's, The Alligator Lounge, Spaceland, Luna Park, Largo, the Mint, Harvelles, the Garage, and many more.

MISCELLANEOUS RESTAURANTS

Rebecca's, L.A. Trattoria, James Beach, Louis Quatorze, Mandalay, Mandarette, Maple Drive, Atlas Bar and Grill, El Cholo, Mexica, Muse, Les Dous, the Palm, the Grill, Vida, Red, Cha Cha Cha, Hirozen, Hama Sushi, Dan Tanna's.

RRRRIOT GRRRRL

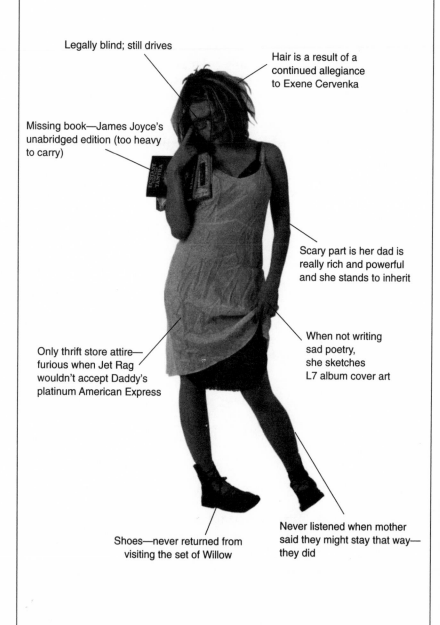

Legally blind; still drives

Hair is a result of a continued allegiance to Exene Cervenka

Missing book—James Joyce's unabridged edition (too heavy to carry)

Scary part is her dad is really rich and powerful and she stands to inherit

Only thrift store attire—furious when Jet Rag wouldn't accept Daddy's platinum American Express

When not writing sad poetry, she sketches L7 album cover art

Shoes—never returned from visiting the set of Willow

Never listened when mother said they might stay that way—they did

PLACES TO SHOP

As you've no doubt learned by now, image is everything. So it's important to know where you can shop for yours. We've compiled a list to help you know your limitations in the buyer's marketplace.

$	Cheap
$$	Reasonable
$$$	Better have a regular job
$$$$	Have a lot of money, or be married to it

UPSCALE

Barneys $$$$ A place where you can rub elbows with Sharon Stone while reaching for the latest Prada or sit next to Kevin Costner while trying on your new Gucci loafers. Even if you can't afford to buy anything, it's a great place to be seen.

Maxfield $$$$ If you're willing to pay for extended sucking up and $600 for a Japanese T-shirt, then this is the place for you.

Fred Segal $$$ Hip, hip, hip. Two locations to serve your every fashion need. Even rock stars are proud to shop here, and no one seems to mind spending five times what anything's worth. They see it as their way of tipping the management.

29

Neiman-Marcus $\boxed{\text{\$\$\$\$}}$ Barneys has stolen a lot of Neiman's thunder, but it's still a great place to valet park.

Rodeo Drive and Rodeo 2 $\boxed{\text{\$\$\$\$\$}}$ It may be a little confusing at first, but no, you're not in Tokyo. After all, photo ops are aplenty, and why not get in some shopping while you're at it? Every major fashion house is represented. You can spend enough to feed Rwanda and Sally Struthers in that two-block radius.

HIP

Agnes B $\boxed{\text{\$\$\$}}$ The B would seem to stand for black, bored, or bitchy, since everything in the store is dark colors, which seems to have a negative effect on the help. We're convinced they import all the people that work there from New York or Paris. This place takes the phrase "you can never be too rich or too thin" to new heights.

Fred Segal $\boxed{\text{\$\$\$}}$ So hip we have to mention it twice.

Rampage (Beverly Center) $\boxed{\text{\$\$}}$ If you're over eighteen, don't try on any of the powder blue stretch pants unless you brought a gun and feel suicidal. Nevertheless, this is certainly the place to shop in order to look cool and still be able to afford the cover charge at the Viper Room later that night.

J. Crew $\boxed{\text{\$\$}}$ For that "it's not about the outside, it's about who you are inside" look. Once reserved for preppies, now anyone can look right while walking their golden retriever on the beach.

The Gap $$ You may have to look hard, but you can find some hip things here. If you don't feel like driving to J. Crew in Pasadena, you can get away with Gap khakis.

Banana Republic $$ Yet another variation of J. Crew and the Gap.

GRUNGE

Thrift Stores $ Melrose, Venice, and La Brea are your best bets for those RRRRIOT GRRRRL and BOYYYY looks.

ON DRIVING

N ow that you've landed in Hollywood, your most essential purchase is definitely a car. Not only is it the only way to function in this giant suburb that passes for a city, but it will one day be the very symbol of your personal success.

If you're here to get into the movie or music industries, since they're the only real reasons to be here (obviously Florida has the sweeter oranges), we must inform you that all the major studios and record companies seem to have been placed about twenty miles apart. There's some speculation that casting directors and agents actually make bets about how quickly you can dress, maneuver through gridlocked traffic, and arrive unflappable for your scheduled appointment.

In any event, you should consider getting a car before you get an apartment. A car can serve as both,

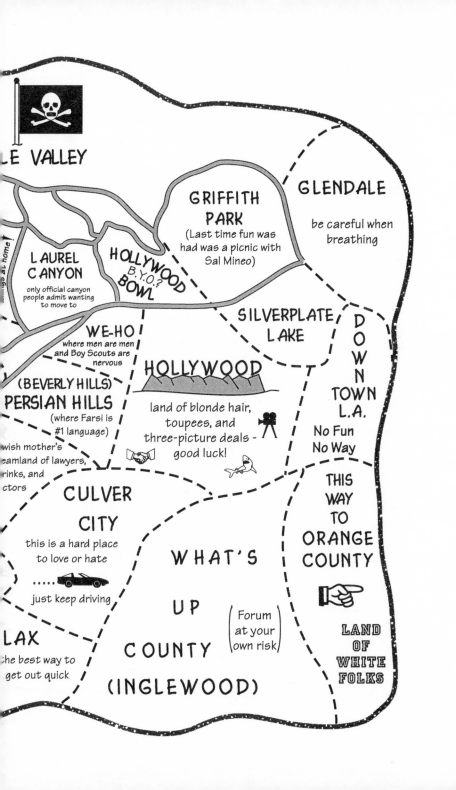

and you can always date to take care of the showering thing.

Once you have your car, you should buy a trusty Thomas Guide to help you get to know your way around. A subtle warning: Don't drive in the rain. Angelenos are used to hot, dry weather conditions. The slightest drizzle can cause deep concern, and fog can bring on overwhelming, terrifying panic. Like sleds on a glacier, cars careen completely out of control as their drivers attempt to steer with one hand while cradling their car phones on their shoulders and applying mascara in the rear view mirror at the same time. After all, isn't that what the rear view mirror is for?

Another tip: parking. Practically impossible to find, and it is almost necessary to carry a knapsack full of quarters with you at all times, otherwise you'll end up paying more in parking tickets than you did for your car. Make sure you check the street signs—you don't want to come out and find your car's been towed. As expensive as that is, you may end up just letting them keep it.

Your archenemies will be known as the 405, the 10, and the 101. No matter what time of day, or what day, these freeways are always jammed. Try finding alternate routes in your Thomas Guide. It will be a day well spent.

At any rate, you will soon figure out all the nuances of driving. We don't need to go into that. What's most important is not *how* you drive, but *what* you drive.

CAR DO'S, DON'TS, AND ACCEPTABLE MAYBE'S

DO'S	DON'TS	ACCEPTABLE MAYBE'S
A-list		
Corniche	Chrysler LeBaron	Anything goes if
Ferrari	Toyota Celica	you're cute
Mercedes (C-class	Volkswagen Fox	enough
or convertible)	Camaros and	
Bentley	Firebirds (unless	
BMW	you have big hair	
Citröen	and live in the	
Jaguar	Valley)	
Any vintage classic	Chevrolets (except	
(over $50,000 in	Corvettes)	
acceptable trade)	Anything red	
such as a 1957	Anything '70s	
T-Bird	(unless you're	
Porsche	eighteen and it's a	
Range Rover	convertible Bug)	
Hummer (driven	Anything '80s	
with a cigar in	(unless it's a	
your mouth)	convertible)	
B-list	Anything with	
	missing parts and	
Saab	homemade paint	
Audi	job	
Volvo	Nothing souped up	
Lexus	unless it's a prop	
Cadillac	car from *La*	
Any 4-wheel drive	*Bamba*	
Any convertible		
(except Chrysler		
LeBaron)		

A final word on driving: Remember the importance of looking good at stoplights, at stop signs, and in parking lots. This can advance your career, enhance your sex life, change your living situation, or, at the very least, get you a dinner and a gimlet at the Ivy (in town).

7
STOPLIGHT PICK-UP TIPS

1 Never get caught with your fingers near your nose.

2 It's a good time to seductively apply lip gloss.

3 Look quickly, and determine whether you could spend Thanksgiving with his/her family. If so, mouth the words "pull over."

4 Decide whether your cars are compatible.

5 If he/she is in a better car and winks at you, you must be having a good hair day.

6 Check for out-of-state plates—it's not worth putting any work into a long-distance relationship.

7 If the person's really cute, even the lawnmower in back of his/her truck shouldn't matter.

7 STEPS TO GETTING A BETTER CAR

1 Flirting: good for temporary use of just about any vehicle they have access to (keep in mind, the deal must be closed soon, or you're back to walking).

2 Heavy Petting: This can get you a luxury rental for at least a week.

3 Just Shy of Penetration: will get you lunch at the Ivy, and use of his company's limousine at your leisure.

4 Lip Aerobics: Depending on your talent and your frequency (and ability to tolerate), you could get a six-month, short-term lease with airline mileage kickbacks and a convertible top (even if the relationship fizzles, you have it until the lease runs out).

5 Occasional Penetration Accompanied by Pillow Talk: Two-year lease with options (and driving gloves thrown in for style).

6 Frequent Sex, Personal Belongings at Their House, and Dinner with Mother: Your own car in their name.

7 Three Ways with Latex, Leather, and Toys: You can drive anything, and it's in your name. **CONGRATULATIONS!**

CAREER CHOICES

The first career opportunity that will be available to you will most likely be in the restaurant industry (i.e., waiter, waitress, bartender, hostess). Unless, of course, you have a master's degree—then perhaps you can fight for a position in an agency mailroom. Below we have outlined some qualifications you need to achieve your lifelong dreams.

ACTOR/ACTRESS

acting (n.), art or occupation of performing parts in plays, films, etc.

actor/actress (n.), one who acts

qualifications: lots of ego and narcissism, constant need for attention, utter selfishness, lack of loyalty

---

OUT-OF-WORK ACTOR GUY

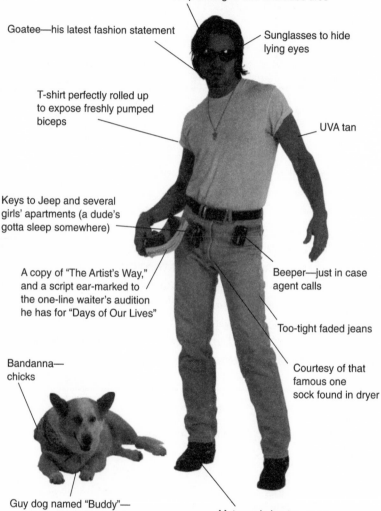

Tossled hair from riding around in Jeep Wrangler with oversized tires

Goatee—his latest fashion statement

Sunglasses to hide lying eyes

T-shirt perfectly rolled up to expose freshly pumped biceps

UVA tan

Keys to Jeep and several girls' apartments (a dude's gotta sleep somewhere)

A copy of "The Artist's Way," and a script ear-marked to the one-line waiter's audition he has for "Days of Our Lives"

Beeper—just in case agent calls

Too-tight faded jeans

Bandanna—chicks

Courtesy of that famous one sock found in dryer

Guy dog named "Buddy"—prop for back of Jeep and to pick up girls at the beach (chicks love the dog)

Motorcycle boots—even though he doesn't own a bike, they're just cool

Obviously, you must have had the lead in your high school play, and once you felt the adulation from that entire standing auditorium filled with your friends and relatives, you knew you were meant for the bigtime. There was no stopping you. Let's just hope that wasn't the zenith of your career and that you have some real potential. In that case, we're going to outline some prerequisites for the difficult journey in front of you.

It's important to set aside any scruples you may once have had. You must learn to lie without guilt or reservation. You weren't in your high school play—you were in the off-Broadway revival of *Our Town*. Always drop your age by a good ten years. If you're eighteen, you're 8—but you can play older. Immediately enroll in an acting class. Personally, we recommend any class with a lot of good-looking models in which the dating potential is strong, since that is the real reason for scene-study. (Also, class is one way of networking and finding out what's going on in the industry.)

You will need head shots. A school photo ID will not do. We're talking 8×10 black and white. One way to find a photographer (and a date at the same time) is to look at the pictures of the other actors/actresses in your class, and then ask to be introduced to the photographer who took the photos. Hopefully, you can sleep with the photographer and get a decent rate. Of course, the only thing we can guarantee is that you will get lucky (and we're not talking about the photo fee).

You will need a résumé to accompany your head shots. Your résumé should be padded with lots of credits and training, none of which you actually have. Keep your credits obscure, or make sure you have a backup lie for each and every one. For example, if you put down a guest shot on "Baywatch" on your résumé and someone you meet casts for "Baywatch" and doesn't remember you, simply reply that it was "San Francisco Baywatch," a little-known series about a small group of scantily clad fishermen. See what we mean? It's easy.

Next, you will need a SAG (Screen Actors Guild) card. This is your passport for getting into the profession, but it is much more difficult to get than, say, a Cuban visa. This is the only time we would suggest sleeping with the producer or becoming an extra (something we hope you have to do only once). In the end, though, it's worth it to get that little rectangular key to a life of perpetual rejection. Your SAG card is, in essence, your identity. Don't leave home without it.

Rejection is par for the course, so don't let it get you down. You know that you are the demigod that your mother raised—they just haven't figured it out yet. You are a horse with blinders, running for the silver cup, and no unimaginative casting director will deter you from your goal. This attitude should get you through at least a couple of auditions.

MODEL

modeling (n.), to display clothing by wearing it

model (n.), one who models

qualifications: pretty face, good body, empty mind

You decided to pursue your career in modeling after a successful debut for Casual Corner at your local mall. Under your picture in your high school yearbook were the words "Our own Christie Brinkley." It didn't matter that the pickings were slim—you took it seriously. So here you are, local beauty contest ribbons in hand, ready to conquer the fashion world.

First of all, if you truly were tall, thin, beautiful, and vapid, you would be in New York or Paris, or, at the very least, Milan. Obviously you're missing one of those four prerequisites. So accept the fact that what you've really come here to be is a MAW (Model/Actress/Whatever). Fine. We can work with that. In fact, 90 percent of the people in Hollywood have to work with that.

We'll let you in on a not-very-well-kept secret, one which everyone in the industry knows. Two words: breast enhancement. Breast enhancement is the cornerstone in the success of every famous pin-up girl in the industry. If you're lacking in the cash department, the Wonderbra is a safe short-term investment. The majority of the work in Hollywood consists of wearing a bikini and holding something out of a mechanic's toolbox, so understand this: Nothing you're holding should be hiding your chest.

Now you're going to need an agency. There are two types of agencies in this town: legitimate and not so legitimate. The first is easy to spot. You will be unmercifully dissected from head to toe from the moment you walk in to the moment you leave. Despite the insults, however, the agency people must feel they can get you work and make themselves money. To them you are a commodity, not a person.

There are quite a few disreputable agencies, in fact, more than those that are reputable. Here are a few red flags to look out for:

1. The agency is located in the spare room of someone's apartment.

MODEL/ACTRESS/WHATEVER (MAW)

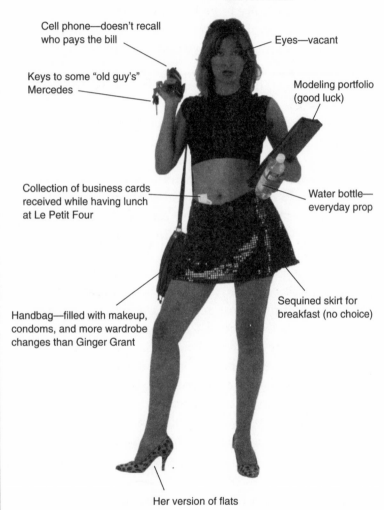

Sunglasses used as headband and root check

Cell phone—doesn't recall who pays the bill

Eyes—vacant

Keys to some "old guy's" Mercedes

Modeling portfolio (good luck)

Collection of business cards received while having lunch at Le Petit Four

Water bottle— everyday prop

Handbag—filled with makeup, condoms, and more wardrobe changes than Ginger Grant

Sequined skirt for breakfast (no choice)

Her version of flats

2. The agency consists of a seedy-looking guy with a video camera.

3. There is a sign in the agency's waiting room that reads "Please remove all unnecessary clothing."

4. The agency suggests you do some test shots with Charles Rathbun—he might be hard to get hold of, but he charges only for film and developing.

5. The agency requests a cash deposit to ensure that they remember who you are whenever you call the office.

AGENT

agent (n.), one who acts for another in business, politics, etc.

qualifications: no heart or soul, predatory instincts, incessant need to control

---

If you want to be an agent, you must be a pathological liar. It would help if you had a law degree, but that is secondary and can be avoided if you possess the utter ruthlessness it takes to claw your way to the top. Lying, cheating, backstabbing, stealing—every defect you were taught to avoid in childhood are the very qualities that will become your virtues.

First of all, you will probably start off in the mailroom, where you will be summarily ignored, abused, and berated. Get used to it. After that, if you're lucky, you will be in a position to do the same to subsequent lowly mailroom workers. After the mailroom, you will move up to assistant to the assistant of an agent. Now you can pound your chest with pride. Hopefully, by

HOLLYWOOD AGENT

Feels good about his hair. It's thick and here to stay!

Paranoid about ear hair

Likes shirts with extra starch on collar, med on cuffs, light down the front, heavy on back tail, none across shoulders, etc., etc. . .

Actually prefers 7-Eleven coffee

This scream is to his mom (it could be about anything)

Out of frustration is locking and unlocking his Porsche

Knee pads were custom-made not to show!

Drove the tailor at Barneys crazy for two weeks deciding whether or not to have cuffs!

Wears lifts!

the time you are thirty-five, you will be an agent. If, however, you are not afraid to display your sharklike maneuvering and trounce on people as you climb to the top, then you may succeed at a much earlier age. Now that you're an agent and you have some clients, you find yourself attending screenings, parties, all the events. Your ass is being kissed, you don't have enough time to return all your phone calls, and you can't remember the last time you told the truth. You have a company car phone in your company BMW, a company credit card, a company wife and children, and company accounts at Morton's and the Ivy. Life is fantastic.

How did this happen? Let's go back to some of the fundamental skills that helped you acquire your clients. When you first met, it was like magic. They could see their new celebrity lifestyle reflected in your eyes. You were as hungry as they were. In their souls, they just knew that you'd kill for them and they'd never be implicated, that you would be available to them for anything, at any hour. Sweet nothings were whispered—things like "you're a real artist; a natural; innovative; star quality; raw genius"—and they believed you. And you knew they would, because in your heart you really felt that they were all a bunch of narcissistic wackos at best, most suffering from multiple-personality disorders—you know Nicolas Cage didn't pull those characters out of thin air. But it's a match made in Heaven. They're self-involved, and you're a sociopath with a law degree.

WRITER

write (v.), to scribe literary works for publishing, motion pictures, or television

writer (n.), one who writes

qualifications: brilliance, sophistication, complete humility, selflessness, warm nature

OR

qualifications: cynicism, alcoholism, suicidal depression, self-loathing, bipolar disorder

---

Always remember, as far as everyone else in the industry is concerned, as a writer, you are invisible. Merely a nuisance to deal with on the way to get their dream project made. The script obviously materialized in front of them as a result of their sudden visualization one day. If it's a success, you can be sure they'll thank their psychic before they do you.

On your way to becoming a member of the Writer's Guild, get used to hearing things such as:

1. It's just not high concept enough.

2. If only we can attach it to the right star.

3. If only we can attach it to the right director.

4. Can you rewrite it so it doesn't have so much annoying social relevance, and also pad it with a lot more gratuitous action?

5. Can you make the female lead an ex-hooker with lots of flashbacks of her pole-dancing? I mean, who knows what Mother Teresa did before she entered the nunnery?

50

6. We don't want the dialogue to be more important than the sound track.

7. Demi Moore expressed some interest, but she likes the male lead better. We could make it sort of a nineties *Yentl.* We could call it *Gentl.*

These are just some of the things you will hear before your first screenplay ever gets sold. Plod on, don't lose hope (at least not yet). If you can be flexible, you can actually have a successful career. Don't worry that people won't know your name—you're a writer, and that's normal. They just think there's only one guy who churns out every script in Hollywood, and his name is Joe Eszterhas.

Enjoy your acclimation into the land of the unknown. Financially, it's great, but if you're in it for the fame, find a new career. Just remember, without you, it's mime.

PUBLICIST

publicity (n.), information given out to attract public attention to a person, cause, etc.

publicist (n.), a person in the publicity business, especially a press agent

qualifications: gift of gab, excellent creative writing skills, great imagination, at least fifteen different ways to say "no comment"

Does the saying "You can't make a silk purse from a sow's ear" mean anything to you? It will, because from now on, that's what you'll be doing for a living.

PUBLICIST

Inner child is a tall blonde who once dated Johnny Depp

Bisexual haircut—not too short, not too long

Once swallowed an entire mouthful of ink in client meeting

Always says "Never point"

Working with therapist to release clipboard

Exact suit purchased by Kate Capshaw, according to designer

After many hours with trainer (6 years), finally has confidence to expose tummy

Insists shoes weren't bought to increase height— "Just liked the style"

Not just any sow, either, but rich, famous spoiled sows with huge egos. It will be your job to make them look like the best silk purses their money can buy. If they dare see one single item that reveals them rolling in slop, you're fired. You're in marketing, and the product you're selling is image. And in Hollywood, image is everything.

Let's face it. How many parents would want their kids to play with Barbie if they knew what was really going on in that dream house of hers? Poor Skipper. Horrible drug problem. Oh, so you thought she was just discontinued? Nope. Long-term rehab. And Ken? Gay as the day is long. Didn't you notice when he started wearing those mesh shirts, tight pants, and a little too much jewelry? Oh, and Barbie. Obviously anorexic. We hear she even had a couple of ribs removed to give her that tiny little waist. See, and you never knew. Why? Great publicist. You always see Barbie and Ken out and about together, holding hands, dressed to perfection—the happy, healthy celebrity couple. What you don't see is the hardworking person who makes sure their dirty little designer laundry never gets aired. And that person can be *you*.

PRODUCER

produce (v.), to get (a play, motion picture, etc.) organized for public presentation

producer (n.), one who produces

qualifications: money (preferably someone else's), leased offices, business cards, fancy name on door such as F.L.A.S.H. (Film Label Accession Scheming Headquarters) Productions, Armani suit, master manipulation skills

---

So you went to Cornell and studied business. But you still had a flaky disposition left over from that Bohemian prep school you attended. Not good enough to get you that CEO position at a major corporation, as Mom and Dad would've liked, but just the right credentials to become a Hollywood producer. The idea occurred to you after seeing an interview with your newfound idol, Joel Silver, and his great body of work, the formula action movie. You were the king of grade school antics after that cherry-bomb-in-the-trash-can incident, and you talked your way not only out of detention but also into the next grade. You were destined even then.

Now you're in Hollywood. You convinced Mom and Dad to back your brilliant stock scheme, which was quickly abandoned for a convertible Porsche, some Armani suits, a Beverly Hills office, and a new model girlfriend. Not to worry—Dad's accountant won't figure it out until next tax season, and by then you'll have your first hit movie under your belt.

You may have to start out doing a few Billy Zane/Lara Flynn Boyle movies, but most producers start out that way. You could, however, get a leg up by pretending you're someone's distant relative—Warner, Cohn, Mayer—names common enough not to get found out. No matter what, they'll take your calls and probably read your project in the hopes of meeting your famous relative. It will also get you into all of those important parties that you will need to attend, as that is most of your job. By the way, the model girlfriend comes in handy here. Not only will she make you look good, but you can trade her off for a future connection. Remember, envy is power—and it's great when you've got it to give away.

You completely perplexed your high school guidance counselor after hours of agonizing over the endless career choices that lay ahead when she realized there was not a single one that suited you. The only thing she kept saying over and over again was how great you looked, but short of that, you had no other skills. You did have a fair share of wit to get you through, however. What to do but work with what you've got, and where to go to polish that image? You knew that in New York, you'd just be one of the crowd, but in Hollywood, you'd be a standout in any room.

Keep in mind, most of your backing will come from either your grandmother or that trust fund Mom and Dad set up for you after kindergarten when they realized you would never amount to anything. Luckily, they loved you and had the necessary parental guilt. Good thing you weren't a Kennedy, and lobotomy wasn't an option.

Your job is to be seen at parties and clubs. Period. Nothing else. Your days will be spent sleeping, sunning, or shopping. The evenings (pre-dinner) will be spent receiving phone calls about where and when the parties are and who will be there, followed by changing clothes and endless primping. It would also be nice if you had someone there—friend, neighbor, paid companion—to tell you how great you look after each hair and wardrobe decision.

This career choice isn't as expensive as it may seem since you rent, well, everything—car, apartment, dates. So if things get a little out of control, you can just return it all the next day and go home to live with Grandma. But if you look good, have the funds, and have great hair, you're there.

THE FIVE-YEAR PLAN TO GETTING WHAT YOU WANT

Producer

FIRST THREE MONTHS: Personal trainer

FIRST YEAR: Hairdresser (if you trim the right star)

THIRD YEAR: Producer (your deal with the Japanese should only result in movies with pretty boys in fast planes who are sexually confused)

FOURTH YEAR: Studio head (you're so powerful that you can write off your newly acquired drug habit on the books)

FIFTH YEAR: Dead (with hooker and nose full of fun!)

Actor/Actress

FIRST THREE MONTHS: Still have your own money, a good outlook, and the nose you were born with

FIRST YEAR: A job at Morton's (waiting tables), a good head shot, and a new nose

THIRD YEAR: A job at Morton's (assistant manager), dating a studio exec who has promised you a part in the next Van Damme movie

57

FOURTH YEAR: No longer at Morton's except to dine in front part of the room, currently sleeping with any producer who has that perfect vehicle for you

FIFTH YEAR: Nominated for an Academy Award (Best Supporting Role), house in hills (leased), and paparazzi on your payroll to generate interest when dining publicly

Musician/Composer

FIRST THREE MONTHS: Cocaine dealer

FIRST YEAR: Still a cocaine dealer, now with an all-access pass to any concert or recording studio

THIRD YEAR: In rehab writing songs with a major player from Crosby, Stills and Nash

FOURTH YEAR: Song you wrote in rehab is now a big hit with hip young girl singer on a good label

FIFTH YEAR: Grammy, Grammy, Grammy, and your own record deal, not to mention your own private cocaine dealer

Agent

FIRST THREE MONTHS: Prostitute/mailroom person at large agency

FIRST YEAR: Assistant to bigwig, with current dirt on all the hot stars

THIRD YEAR: Married to big star with your own separate sex lives and a baby on the way

FIFTH YEAR: Running agency, divorced from big star, and buying a puppy

Writer/Director

FIRST THREE MONTHS: Depressed

FIRST YEAR: Still in bed

THIRD YEAR: Your script made it to Quentin Tarantino's company, but he wants to star in and direct it

FOURTH YEAR: Signed the deal with Quentin, and back in bed feeling like a sellout

FIFTH YEAR: Living in Australia with a huge FedEx bill that you can pay because of all the rewrite jobs you've gotten, and questioning whether outback gear will be acceptable at the Oscars

Publicist

FIRST THREE MONTHS: Fat, single

FIRST YEAR: Fatter, but has now learned the importance of the removal of unwanted hair and a job as an assistant at a hot firm

THIRD YEAR: Straightened hair, capped teeth, and Tom Hanks's home phone number, still single

FOURTH YEAR: Deal with Disney, still fat after all those spa trips with Oprah

FIFTH YEAR: Third name in partnership of company, really cute young boyfriend on allowance and short leash, still fat

Model

FIRST THREE MONTHS: Practicing your signature

FIRST YEAR: Sleeping your way to a better portfolio

THIRD YEAR: New chest, sleeping your way to a better car

FOURTH YEAR: New lips, sleeping your way to a better house

FIFTH YEAR: Black eye, mulatto baby, ticket back to Oklahoma

Poseur

FIRST THREE MONTHS: Looking good and a wallet full of Dad's credit cards

FIRST YEAR: Still looking good and lunches with Cathy Lee Crosby at Cafe Med

THIRD YEAR: Less hair from stress, still lunching with Cathy Lee Crosby at Cafe Med

FOURTH YEAR: Bitter that you're still lunching with Cathy Lee Crosby at Cafe Med

FIFTH YEAR: Living in Key West running a bicycle shop, E-mailing Cathy Lee Crosby, and weighing three hundred pounds

THE ASSISTANT

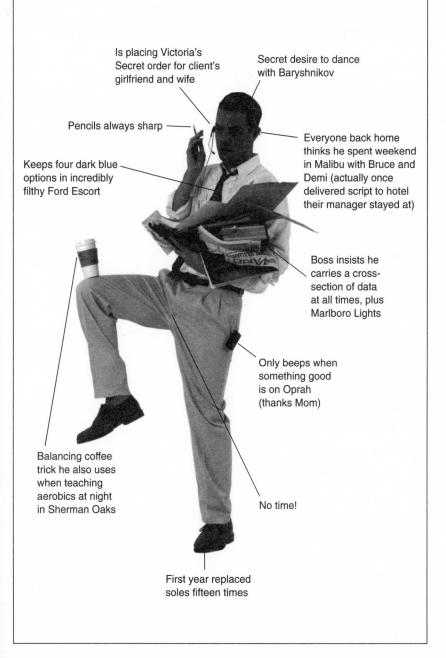

Is placing Victoria's Secret order for client's girlfriend and wife

Secret desire to dance with Baryshnikov

Pencils always sharp

Keeps four dark blue options in incredibly filthy Ford Escort

Everyone back home thinks he spent weekend in Malibu with Bruce and Demi (actually once delivered script to hotel their manager stayed at)

Boss insists he carries a cross-section of data at all times, plus Marlboro Lights

Only beeps when something good is on Oprah (thanks Mom)

Balancing coffee trick he also uses when teaching aerobics at night in Sherman Oaks

No time!

First year replaced soles fifteen times

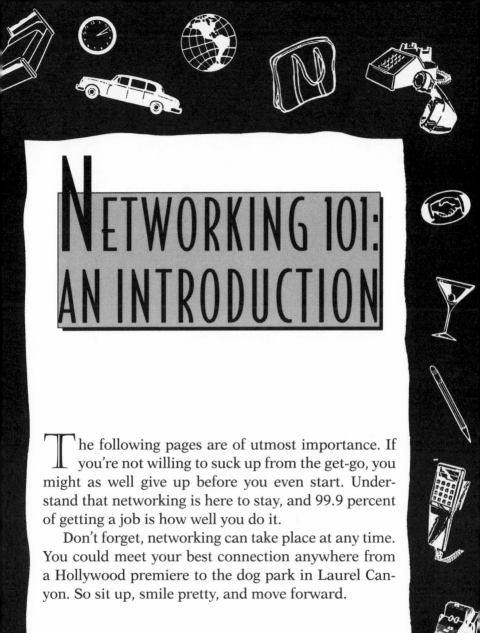

NETWORKING 101: AN INTRODUCTION

The following pages are of utmost importance. If you're not willing to suck up from the get-go, you might as well give up before you even start. Understand that networking is here to stay, and 99.9 percent of getting a job is how well you do it.

Don't forget, networking can take place at any time. You could meet your best connection anywhere from a Hollywood premiere to the dog park in Laurel Canyon. So sit up, smile pretty, and move forward.

10 WAYS TO GET A STUDIO DEAL

1 Know what that means.

2 Hang out at a cigar store and get chummy with any customer in an Armani suit.

3 Do whatever it takes with the guard at the studio gate to get a drive-on pass.

4 Become a bookie, drug dealer, or hooker (if all of the above, the Japanese will call you directly).

5 Date Barbra Streisand, period.

6 Date David Geffen if you're better at that.

7 Sleep with a studio head's ugly offspring and fasten your seatbelt for a quick ride to the top.

8 Develop a pretentious foreign accent.

9 Develop a script with a fresh new look at the Holocaust.

10 Find the ugliest, shortest, most repulsive, unattached studio executive. Pimp for him, and make sure you're hired and given shares right before he makes that multi-million-dollar merger.

10 WAYS TO NOT GET A STUDIO DEAL

1 Know what that means.

2 Spend your down time at the Bodhi Tree Bookstore.

3 Accept a walk-on pass (after the guard sees you in your rusted AMC Pacer).

4 Date a bookie, drug dealer, or hooker.

5 Date Elliott Gould.

6 Stop dating David Geffen.

7 Reject a studio head's ugly offspring, and you will keep making those nonfat lattes for those dieting Beverly Hills housewives.

8 Have a Persian accent.

9 Pitch *Easy Rider IV* starring Gary Busey and Jan-Michael Vincent (this may backfire and actually get you a deal, so be prepared).

10 Option a really good script and believe in it.

10 WAYS TO GET INTO A PARTY TO WHICH YOU'RE NOT INVITED

1 Crash and hope you blend in.

2 The night before the party, sleep with someone who's been invited.

3 Drop the name of the person giving the party, and hope that that's not who you're talking to.

4 Add the name Kennedy to yours and hope for the best; after all, there are lots of relatives (they're Catholic).

5 Become a drug dealer.

6 Pretend you're a liquor delivery person, then hide in a spare room.

7 Say, "I'm with Jack Nicholson and he'll be arriving shortly." They'll be too afraid to turn you away, and Jack won't care if he invited you or not.

8 Get a job with a caterer, bring a change of clothes, and quit halfway through the party.

9 Name-drop until the person with the guest list is so exhausted that they let you in out of frustration.

10 Be really cute.

10 WAYS TO LOSE YOUR PARTY INVITATION

1 Tell them you're bringing Fabio.

2 Tell them you're bringing Fabio and Shannen Doherty.

3 Tell them you're bringing Fabio, Shannen Doherty, and Anna Nicole Smith.

4 Tell them you're bringing Fabio, Shannen Doherty, Anna Nicole Smith, and Sean Young.

5 Tell them you're bringing Fabio, Shannen Doherty, Anna Nicole Smith, Sean Young, and Dennis Woodruff.

6 Tell them you're bringing Fabio, Shannen Doherty, Anna Nicole Smith, Sean Young, Dennis Woodruff, and Angelyne.

7 Tell them you're bringing Fabio, Shannen Doherty, Anna Nicole Smith, Sean Young, Dennis Woodruff, Angelyne, and Pauly Shore.

8 Tell them you're bringing Fabio, Shannen Doherty, Anna Nicole Smith, Sean Young, Dennis Woodruff, Angelyne, Pauly Shore, and Kato Kaelin.

9 Tell them you're bringing Fabio, Shannen Doherty, Anna Nicole Smith, Sean Young, Dennis Woodruff, Angelyne, Pauly Shore, Kato Kaelin, and La Toya Jackson.

10 Tell them you're bringing Fabio, Shannen Doherty, Anna Nicole Smith, Sean Young, Dennis Woodruff, Angelyne, Pauly Shore, Kato Kaelin, LaToya Jackson, and anyone from *Baywatch Nights*.

TOP 10 PICK-UP LINES

1 "Excuse me, I'm lost. You must be a model."

2 "Excuse me, I'm lost. You must be an actress/ actor."

3 "Excuse me, I'm lost. Has anyone ever told you that you look like Michelle Pfeiffer/Tom Cruise (or any other beautiful megastar)."

4 "Excuse me, I'm lost. I'm a producer, and I'd like to bring you in on something I'm casting."

5 "Excuse me, I'm lost. You look so familiar. Didn't you do an episode of *Baywatch*?"

6 "Excuse me, I'm lost. I wouldn't have put you a day over eighteen."

7 "Excuse me, I'm lost. You must never get off the Stairmaster; which gym do you go to?"

8 "Excuse me, I'm lost. You're the first brunette I've met—you must color your hair."

9 "Excuse me, I'm lost. You have the most beautiful brown eyes I've ever seen—those must be contacts."

10 "Excuse me, I'm lost. I never get out. Why don't we go to your place?"

NETWORKING 101: SCENARIOS

Actor/Actress

You are at a Hollywood party that another waiter/waitress invited you to. Your friend hasn't arrived yet, so you chat with the bartender. A tall, attractive man/woman walks up and introduces himself/herself. After striking up a conversation, you tell him/her your name and explain how awkward you feel about not knowing anyone at the party and being new in town. When he/she asks you what you do, you say you hope to be an actress/actor. The person tells you he/she is a writer and asks you for your phone number, which you happily jot down on a cocktail napkin, stating how much you would love to see him/her again.

WHAT'S WRONG WITH THE ABOVE SCENARIO?

1. Never accept an invitation from another waiter/waitress. You are not here to make friends, you are here to win. (See "10 Ways to Get Into a Party to Which You're Not Invited," page 66.)

2. There should be no reason to speak to the bartender unless you're asking for a drink or directions to a better party.

3. No one with any power in this town is tall and attractive, and in the rare exception to that rule, he/she would already be in the company of several beautiful men/women and would have no reason to talk to you.

4. Always introduce yourself by adding -stein, -berg, -feld, or -blatt to your last name.

5. Never say you don't know anyone at a party. You always know everyone and are just disappointed that Tom and Nicole haven't arrived yet, because when you saw them earlier at Bruce and Demi's beach party, they said they'd be following shortly.

6. You never hope to be an actor/actress—you are a film artiste who may sell out to the commercial world of television, but only for the financial freedom to do what you really want to do, which is to direct Ibsen.

7. Writers can do nothing for you.

8. Never give out your number; ask for a business card.

9. Never be enthusiastic. At all times, your attitude should be one of general boredom.

Musician

You drive up in your Volvo, handing the keys to the valet. You brush your fingers through your shiny, neatly coiffed hair and give a tug on your J. Crew khakis, smiling and waving as you make your way into the party. Once inside, you politely ask the door attendant where you might procure a mineral water. Mineral water in hand, you approach a friend you see who works at Tower Records and ask him if he'd like to play tennis over the weekend. A joint is being passed and you politely decline, pointing to your "Just Say No" button on the pocket of your Members Only jacket. Someone in the group asks you what you play, and you say you play bass in one of the busiest touring party bands. As you're leaving, someone invites you to a party for Porno for Pyros. You decline, saying you never miss Leno, and have never heard of that band anyway.

WHAT'S WRONG WITH THE ABOVE SCENARIO?

1. Volvo? No, no, no. A Harley or a van (but only if you're a drummer).

2. Your hair should always be unkempt, following the musician's rule: You shower only when you have someone else to wash your hair for you.

3. Khakis should never be a part of your wardrobe—Levi's or leather pants only.

4. Smiling and waving on the way in? Never. You are morose, angst-ridden, and annoyed at all times.

5. You don't ask for anything. Go and *take* the bottle of *whiskey* off the bar to guzzle haplessly.

6. The only reason to speak to someone who works at Tower Records is to ask how your CD is selling, and you'd never do that at a party.

ROCKER AND GIRLFRIEND PROP

Once rode an elevator with Springsteen—she refers to it as a "relationship"

Sunglasses: hasn't seen pupils since 1978—thinks eyes could be brown but doesn't care

Breakfast

The one thing holding her up

Braless T-shirt easily lifted, her way of saying "Hi"

Bellychain— usually worn as sole article of clothing

Keys to Harley and NA chip he forgot to remove after latest slip

Tattoo—doesn't know she has it yet

Only memories of "Glam-Rock" days

Man's biker boots, stolen from Axl (he passed out)

7. The closest you've ever come to a tennis racket is air guitar.

8. You not only take the joint, you ask if anyone's got smack.

9. Members Only is to fashion what Michael Bolton is to music.

10. Bass players don't get laid, and party bands only get laid by bridesmaids in a blackout.

11. First of all, if you don't know who a hip band is, keep it to yourself and get the CD. Second of all, no one watches Leno.

Professional Poseur

You arrive at the party in your reliable old Pinto, which you decide to self-park to save the extra couple of bucks it would take to tip the valet. Always the thrifty one. You're not quite sure who will be at the party, and you have underdressed slightly so you won't stand out in the crowd. Once inside, you spot Madonna, but since you've never met her, you begin to flit nervously around the party, afraid to introduce yourself. As you make your rounds, you chat and point at your famous prey. Madonna picks up on it and promptly asks the hostess to have you escorted out. While being muscled out by two large bodyguards, you wave and shout how much you loved *Shanghai Surprise*. After you leave the party, you realize your Pinto has been towed. On your way back in to request use of the phone, you see Courtney Love. You tell her that you know she had nothing

74

to do with Kurt's death, and ask her if she can give you a lift. She punches you in the face and her bodyguards take over from there. You end up getting a ride home in the ambulance, which ends up costing you more than your car was worth in the first place.

WHAT'S WRONG WITH THE ABOVE SCENARIO?

1. You never drive a practical car. You always drive something flashy, even if you're just renting it for the evening.

2. Always valet park. You're a big spender, and always overtip so those around you will see that you're a pillar of generosity.

3. You always review the party list beforehand.

4. Not only do you not underdress, you always wear something designer, so if you mistakenly leave an article of clothing behind, you can ask for it by name.

5. Madonna is a peer, not someone to be afraid of. If you don't say hello, it's only because you can't be bothered. You've always felt more of an allegiance toward Sandra (Bernhard, of course).

6. You don't flit nervously around a party—you strategically place yourself in the most noticeable position in the room, striking a pose that combines ennui with self-importance, knowing your charisma is a magnet.

7. You never point unless it's to send someone to the bar to get a drink for you.

8. The only reason Madonna would speak to the hostess is to ask when you arrived and why you hadn't said hello yet.

9. You never saw *Shanghai Surprise*. No one did.

10. If you leave a party early, it's always because you have something better to go to next, and if the bodyguards were escorting you anywhere, it would be back in, since no one wanted you to leave yet.

11. No one talks to Courtney Love, they only dress like her.

12. The only time you've been in an ambulance was that night your date O.D.'d on Ecstasy.

Producer

You and a guest have been invited to a dinner party at the home of a struggling but brilliant writer friend of yours. You invite your true love from college, who just moved out here for her new job at the ACLU. You've always admired her work with the underprivileged, even though it doesn't pay much.

The invitation says eight o'clock, so you stop off for a bottle of wine and still arrive on time. You two are the first to arrive, so you offer to help set the table.

At dinner, you discuss underground art and Marxism: How sad that Russia is no longer a Communist country—we could have learned a lot from their socialized medicine.

After dinner is over, you decline the good port, opting for coffee instead because your girlfriend doesn't like you to drink a lot. You retire to the living room and carry on another discussion of the wonders of nature. Finally, after everyone else has left, you and your girlfriend go home to meditate before bed.

WHAT'S WRONG WITH THE ABOVE SCENARIO?

1. Not only would you not know any struggling writers, but you would never be going to a dinner party at their house unless it's to steal a script idea.

2. You dumped your college girlfriend years ago—she was too bleeding-heart liberal and poor—besides, the richest girl in town came back on the market.

3. Money is everything.

4. You never arrive on time, you bring nothing, and you offer nothing, least of all help of any kind.

5. You know nothing about Marxism. In fact, you fell asleep during a screening of *Reds*.

6. Why would you want socialized medicine? Your father owns one of the biggest pharmaceutical companies, which is how you could afford to end up in Hollywood in the first place.

7. You start the dinner drinking and end the dinner drinking. Coffee is for the morning and, after that, for wimps who haven't learned the beauty of controlled consumption.

8. You are the first to leave, not the last. After all, you've got to drop off your date so you can meet up with the hooker.

9. The only nature you know about is how much the gardener charges.

10. You always thought *meditate* was another word for *medicate*.

Model

See "Model Networking: Capturing a Star" on page 81, or, if all else fails, get in touch with Heidi Fleiss.

Writer/Director

A friend of yours has snared a gig as a waiter/caterer for the Palm Springs Film Festival. Since he knows you need money and could use the contacts, he hooks you up with a job. You get to work the opening-night banquet, and under your waiter's jacket you have your latest project neatly tucked away, ready to pull out at the first sighting of anyone who looks like they could get your baby made. While working the tables, you chat endlessly with whoever doesn't walk away: about your project, your life's work, which you hope to direct, based on your grandparents' immigration from Austria and the little bread shop they opened in Milwaukee. Across the room you see Martin Scorsese, and you run quickly over to him, dropping trays and spilling coffee on everyone in your path. When you finally reach him, you give him a big hug, call him Marty, and tell him how happy he should be to meet you, since you're the guy and you have the project that is really going to put him on the map.

WHAT'S WRONG WITH THE ABOVE SCENARIO?

1. You'd write for a soap opera before you'd take a waiting job, particularly at a high-profile function. Besides, you don't have the energy to run around—you're always drained from your personal creativity and all the cigarettes you smoke.

2. Your work is sacred—it's kept under lock and key at home and shown only to people who sign a written release.

3. Certainly you would not chat about your project, and for good reason: You're paranoid, paranoid, paranoid.

4. The only movie ever worth making about immigrating from Austria was *The Sound of Music*, and that's only because it had a great song score.

5. If Scorsese saw you running toward him, you'd be taken out, literally, before you got halfway across the room. If you did manage to get near him and uttered "Marty" from your presumptuous little lips, that would be the last thing you'd ever say, since it's hard to speak without your tongue.

THE SUNDANCE MAN

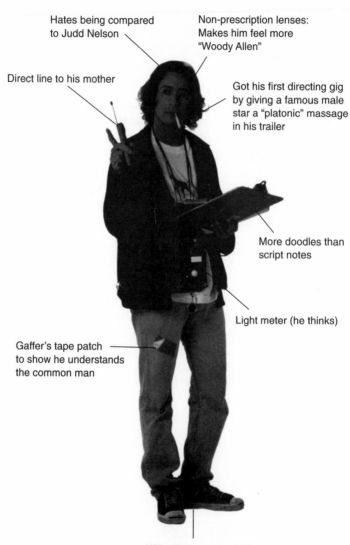

Hates being compared
to Judd Nelson

Non-prescription lenses:
Makes him feel more
"Woody Allen"

Direct line to his mother

Got his first directing gig
by giving a famous male
star a "platonic" massage
in his trailer

More doodles than
script notes

Light meter (he thinks)

Gaffer's tape patch
to show he understands
the common man

Will still be wearing kid's
shoes at 50

MODEL NETWORKING: CAPTURING A STAR

If you don't have the actual talent to become a celebrity, the next best thing is to marry, or at least date, one. There are two ways to be involved with a star. You can sleep with one and, in some cases, even get paid for it. However, getting them to ink your name and phone number in their telephone books is a whole 'nother deal, and the goal of this section.

1. Find someone who knows your star. Subtly manipulate an introduction in a casual setting, preferably at night in dim lighting. If no one you know knows him, you must think creatively. Start reading everything available to get an idea of where you may find your star. For example, if you know he lives in Laurel Canyon, park yourself at the Country Store. Even if your target doesn't show up, you're bound to run into someone famous, and you can't afford to be picky.

2. Don't blow the first meeting—you may never get a second chance. Know his interests. If your star has a fascination with bugs, you're carrying a jar of them. If he is a science fiction fanatic, you're wearing a Ray Bradbury T-shirt. Whatever he likes, coincidentally, you like, too.

3. Once you've arranged a second meeting, don't think you're out of the danger zone. You still have a lot of work ahead of you. Look at Jerry Hall. It took years to get that ring from Mick, and she's a top model. It can be a long and arduous process, but well worth it. Make your second meeting with your star a night he will never forget. Be charming, witty, but not too witty (you wouldn't want him to think you're smarter—they hate that). Dress tastefully, not seductively. Remember, you want him for a lifetime, not a nighttime. Whatever you do, DO NOT SLEEP WITH HIM! Don't be fooled by his easy and immediate intimacy—it's only a test. If you pass, you are on your way. If you don't, you'll be gone in the morning, if not before. Don't even kiss him. You might allow a kiss on the cheek, but that's it.

4. Let's assume you've wrangled a second date. Let's also assume it's going well. You're not eating too much, you haven't gotten drunk, and he hasn't picked up someone else on the way to the bathroom. You are still his date. Conversation is flowing, you are laughing, he is laughing, hands are touching accidentally, all is fantastic. That's your cue that it's time to go home—ALONE. We know that that's not what you want, we're sure that's not what he wants. But understand this: He may want you now, but imagine how much more he'll want you if you say no. He will be wracked with desire and won't be able to get you out of his head. Your phone will probably ring the next day, and then you will be well on your way to date three.

5. The third date is about reeling in your catch, because by now, if you've done all of the above, he's probably caught. Trips will be in the making, you'll be giving him decorating advice, and he'll be telling you how to dress for him. But still, *go home alone.* This will be the last time you'll have to do this. Keep in the back of your mind that they all want a mother, and going home alone is what Mom would do. Grabbing his crotch and begging is a no-no.

6. If you've made it through three dates, you are well on your way to marriage, or at least cohabitation. Given the nature of a celebrity, you have obviously proven yourself to be good at adulation and his favorite subject: himself. You're an expert, and he must have you, because no one knows more about him than you do. He will need to fulfill his need for instant gratification. Don't worry, you're getting something out of it, too. You'll be attending fabulous parties, you will have your picture in the Life/Style section, you will probably see yourself on *Entertainment Tonight* (of course, no one will ever be interviewing you, but your friends and family will know that's you walking behind the megastar), and your wardrobe will vastly improve.

Have fun while it lasts, because it probably won't last long. (Just ask Shoshanna Lonstein.) Let's face it—celebrities have the attention spans of dyslexic fruit flies, so make sure you save all photos.

NEPOTISM: THE NEXT GENERATION

Just when you thought it was safe to be from Dairy-town, U.S.A., be inspired by your high school play, and move to L.A., where you hope to get a part alongside Tom Cruise or Sandra Bullock, enter nepotism, that ugly little connection they call blood-related. Don't even bother trying to compete. It just doesn't work. If you walk into a casting office and you hear the name Arquette or Baldwin called out, forget it. And don't let the door hit you on the way out. But there is a chance that your talent on its own, sans relatives, will land you the part of a lifetime. A slim chance.

Here is a list of your competition. By the way, sometimes nepotism *doesn't* work, as you'll see in List B. Read on.

LIST A: NEPOTISM AT ITS FINEST

Barrymore, Drew, starter John Jr.
Bridges, Jeff and Beau, starter Lloyd
Cage, Nicolas, starter Francis Ford Coppola (uncle)
Carradine, Keith, Robert, and David, starter John
Douglas, Michael, starter Kirk
Downey, Robert Jr., starter Robert Sr.
Farrow, Mia, starter Maureen O'Sullivan
Fisher, Carrie, starters Debbie Reynolds and Eddie
    Fisher

Fonda, Jane, Peter, and Bridget, starter Henry
Grey, Jennifer, starter Joel
Griffith, Melanie, starter Tippi Hedren
Huston, Anjelica, starter John
Minnelli, Liza, starters Judy Garland and Vincente
    Minnelli
O'Neal, Tatum (as a child), starter Ryan
Paltrow, Gwyneth, starters Blythe Danner and Bruce
    Paltrow
Plummer, Amanda, starters Christopher Plummer and
    Tammy Grimes
Redgrave, Vanessa and Lynn, starter Sir Michael
Richardson, Natasha and Joely, starters Vanessa Red-
    grave and director Tony Richardson
Rossellini, Isabella, starters Ingrid Bergman and Ro-
    berto Rossellini
Scott, Campbell, starters George C. Scott and Colleen
    Dewhurst
Sheen, Charlie, and Emilio Estevez, starter Martin
    Sheen
Sorvino, Mira, starter Paul
Stiller, Ben, starters Anne Meara and Jerry Stiller
Sutherland, Kiefer, starter Donald
Tyler, Liv, starter Steven
Weaver, Sigourney, starter Pat (NBC executive)

LIST B: NEPOTISM AT ITS WORST

Bono, Chastity, starters Sonny and Cher
Crosby, Mary, starter Bing
Davis, Patti, starters Ronald Reagan and Nancy Davis
    Reagan
Douglas, Eric, starter Kirk
McQueen, Chad, starter Steve

Phillips, Mackenzie and Chynna and Bijoux (or Bijou),
     starters Michelle and John
Pryor, Rain, starter Richard
Sinatra, Frank Jr., starter Frank Sr.
Wagner, Katie, starter Robert

SIMPLY SIBLINGS

Arquette, Rosanna, Richmond, Alexis, Patricia,
     David—so far
Baldwin, Alec, Billy, Steven, Daniel
Bateman, Justine and Jason
Beatty, Warren, and Shirley MacLaine
Culkin, Macaulay, Kieran, and Quinn—so far
Daly, Tyne and Tim
Dillon, Matt and Kevin
Fontaine, Joan, and Olivia DeHavilland
Gabor, Zsa Zsa and Eva
Gilbert, Melissa and Sara
Graves, Peter, and Arness, James
Lawrence, Joey and brothers
Lowe, Rob and Chad
McNichol, Kristy and Jimmy
Osmonds, too many to mention
Quaid, Dennis and Randy
Roberts, Julia and Eric
Shue, Elisabeth and Andrew
Skye, Ione, and Donovan Leitch
Wayans, Damon, Keenen, Kim, plus more to come
Zappa, Dweezil and Moon

SLEEPING YOUR WAY TO NEPOTISM

Brown, Divine, launching pad Hugh Grant
Capshaw, Kate, launching pad Steven Spielberg
Cox, Courteney, launching pad Michael Keaton
Farrow, Mia, launching pad Frank Sinatra
Hurley, Elizabeth, launching pad Hugh Grant
Keaton, Diane, launching pad Woody Allen
Kidman, Nicole, launching pad Tom Cruise
Irving, Amy, launching pad Steven Spielberg
Love, Courtney, launching pad Kurt Cobain's suicide
Lowe, Rob, launching pad Melissa Gilbert and video-
   tape
Madonna, launching pad Madonna's ego
McGraw, Ali, launching pad Robert Evans
Moore, Demi, launching pad Emilio Estevez; to the
   top, Bruce Willis
Nielsen, Brigitte, launching pad Sylvester Stallone
Otis, Carré, launching pad Mickey Rourke
Peters, Jon, launching pad Barbra Streisand
Previn, Soon Yi, launching pad Woody Allen
Robbins, Tim, launching pad Susan Sarandon
Rogers, Mimi, launching pad Tom Cruise
Schwarzenegger, Arnold, launching pad Maria Shriver
Stevens, Fisher, launching pad Michelle Pfeiffer
Stone, Sharon, launching pad any director she's ever
   worked with

TOP 10 SURVIVAL RULES TO LIVING IN HOLLYWOOD

1 Carry a weapon.

2 Lose the smile, particularly when driving.

3 Never seem too desperate, overeager, or enthusiastic about anything. Remember, it probably won't happen, but at least you have a shot at your dream.

4 Stop dreaming.

5 Always pay your car phone bill (or get someone else to do it).

6 Find a nervous habit, and learn to drive with it.

7 Never be seen shopping at Ross Dress for Less.

8 Avoid Fairfax between Melrose and Third (at all times).

9 Never accept a blind date without a seeing-eye dog.

10 Always have enough money for a bus ticket out of here.

WAYS TO SPOT WINNERS AND LOSERS

WAYS TO AUTOMATICALLY SPOT A LOSER

MALE

1. Gucci-like loafers, Capezios, or Cowboy boots with pants tucked in.

2. Fake Rolex (you can tell by the second hand making jerky movements, as opposed to the smooth, sweeping rotation of the real thing).

3. Heavy cologne.

4. Toothpick use during dinner.

5. Shirt unbuttoned to the navel.

6. Still wearing gold chains and a pinky ring.

7. Colored contact lenses.

8. Flashy business card.

9. Dyed black or spray-on hair, or any other sad attempts to cover baldness.

10. Carries a beeper for no apparent professional reason.

11. Has a cell phone and uses it only to buy cocaine.

12. Leather pants.

13. Bandannas, or walking a dog with a bandanna.

14. Tight pants.

15. Wedding ring, or tan line where wedding ring is supposed to be.

16. Is always scoping the room for greener grass.

17. Discusses your astrological sign.

18. Screams at cab driver, waitress, or anyone else in a menial position.

19. Sulks if you win at anything.

20. Apartment furnished with black lacquer anything.

21. Has mirror above the bed (which has polyester or satin sheets).

22. Says things like "I hated my mother, the whore" and "Women don't like me—I guess I'm a guy's guy."

23. Is pursuing a career as a model.

24. Talks incessantly about ex-mate for the first fifteen minutes.

25. Calls more than once to confirm date.

FEMALE

1. Frequently grabs your arm and laughs hysterically.

2. Goes to the bathroom every few minutes.

3. Carries a beeper for no apparent professional reason.

4. Walks into a party and the whole band knows her name.

5. Is always scoping the room for new sponsors.

6. Lets you know right away she's sober, macrobiotic, and just quit smoking.

7. Fakes endearments, including orgasms.

8. Tight pants with no underwear.

9. Obvious cosmetic surgery.

10. Bookcase is filled entirely with self-help books.

11. Discusses your astrological sign.

12. Talks about being molested as a child.

13. Pursuing a career as a model.

14. Talks incessantly about ex-mate for the first fifteen minutes.

15. Calls more than once to confirm date.

16. Lots of money, no apparent employment.

WAYS TO AUTOMATICALLY SPOT A WINNER (MALE)

WITH MONEY

1. He isn't looking at you.

2. Eats in a quiet corner with Jack Nicholson and Sean Penn and can't be disturbed because they're negotiating.

3. Dresses very uncontrived, in that contrived sort of way.

4. Wears expensive shoes (very expensive).

5. Always gets the front table at Morton's.

6. Instead of carrying a business card and dayplanner, he brings his assistant with him to make appointments.

7. Has at least one sexual harassment suit pending against him.

8. Carries keys to both his in-town and his beach houses, and owns an entire fleet of cars.

9. Just broke up with Julia Roberts or Sharon Stone (but then again, hasn't everyone?).

10. Has no jewelry except for an important antique watch.

. . . AND WHAT YOU'LL HAVE TO TOLERATE

1. Bad sex (and lots of it).

2. Endless conversations about *him*!

3. More bad sex.

4. Always being introduced as his "friend."

5. Bad table manners (this includes laughing at boob jokes being told by his foreign film financier in broken English).

6. His cleaning help comparing you to his last significant other (especially if they liked her).

7. Being nice to his horrible children from his previous marriage to a "major movie star."

8. Gingivitis.

9. An allowance based on the weekend box-office.

10. Sitting in coach while he visits you from first.

WAYS TO AUTOMATICALLY SPOT A WINNER (FEMALE)

WITH MONEY

1. She isn't looking at you.

2. Eats in a quiet corner with Marvin Mitchelson, celebrating her huge settlement.

3. Dresses very uncontrived, in that contrived sort of way.

4. Wears expensive shoes (very expensive).

5. Is tired of sitting at the front table at Morton's.

6. Has a full staff, but is still a gourmet cook.

7. Pretends to like sex.

8. Has her own in-town and beach house, but still prefers her Manhattan apartment.

9. Most recently stole the boyfriends of Julia Roberts and Sharon Stone.

10. Has so much jewelry that she doesn't want any from you.

. . . AND WHAT YOU'LL HAVE TO TOLERATE

1. Fake orgasms.

2. Endless conversations about her ex-husband and the starlet he left her for.

3. More fake orgasms.

4. Always being introduced as her "friend."

5. Only being allowed to enter through the maids quarters after midnight.

6. Dirty looks from the cleaning help.

7. Being nice to her horrible children from the previous marriage to a major movie mogul.

8. Silicone everything.

9. An allowance based on her ex's weekend box-office.

10. Sitting with the nanny in coach while she visits you from first.

TOP 5 AREAS TO LIVE—AND WHY

1. Malibu
   A. You're incredibly famous and they come to see you.
   B. You're incredibly famous and you have a house in town, too.

2. Beverly Hills/Bel Air (north of Sunset)
   A. Because it's really beautiful.
   B. You're incredibly rich, famous, cute, or married well (or all of the above).

3. Brentwood
   A. The land of doctors, lawyers, and laser surgeons.
   B. The land of wives of doctors, lawyers, and laser surgeons.

4. Hollywood Hills/Mulholland
   A. Hollywood Hills: You're rich and you're an "artist."
   B. Mulholland: You're a movie star stud put out to pasture.

5. Venice
   A. You're so chic you don't care who your neighbors are (since most live out of shopping carts).
   B. You're so chic that you like the novelty of mingling with your "neighbors."

TOP 5 AREAS NOT TO LIVE— AND WHY

1. The Valley
   A. Enough said.

2. Anywhere near LAX
   A. Only exception would be if you have no choice or you're hearing-impaired.

3. Wilshire Corrider
   A. Where the rental agreement includes camel parking and finger bells.

4. Downtown L.A.
   A. Don't kid yourself that you need the loft space—you really just need to be near your next fix.

5. Anywhere the word *adjacent* applies
   A. *Adjacent* means "the cool area is my view."
   B. *Adjacent* means "I can't afford the real thing."

THE WHATZ UP, 40 OZ., HIP HOP, VIDEO DIRECTOR, GANGSTA BRO

HEFFER , RAD works 40 BRO Later snags SEXY !

LINGO

(n., pl. **lingoes:** strange or incomprehensible language)

Gangstas

Word, homies, sit up in your cribs, open your audios, and get hip to the vibe I'm throwin' down. You better recognize the 411, cause it is the dope. I'm tellin' ya. Fresh. Cool. Phat. All that—and a bag of chips.

Did you understand anything in the above paragraph? We didn't think so. Basically, it translates as follows: Listen, my friends, while at home be aware and alert and try to understand the importance of what I'm telling you. I'm giving you the information you need to know, and it's great—great, great, great, really great.

Don't worry, we didn't expect you to know that. We didn't know it either when we first got here. But you will soon realize, as we did, how crucial understanding this and other types of slang can be to your new false identity. Once you've mastered this fine art, you can go anywhere and fit right in. Let's say you get lost on the

FLY G PEEPS '' CAKE OPP

airhead tubes REEK epic

way to the Forum and need directions. Remember, you can't talk surfer in the 'hood—they frown on that. However, it's cool to talk gangsta anywhere. Soon all this will be second nature to you, and you'll forget you ever knew English at all. If necessary, start making a cheat sheet that fits in the pocket of your oversized, low-slung chinos.

GANGSTA LEXICON

THE BOMB (adj.), ultimately cool
DOPE (adj.), ultimately cool
FRESH (adj.), ultimately cool
FLY (adj.), ultimately cool
ALL THAT (adj.), ultimately cool
ALL THAT AND A BAG OF CHIPS (adj.), ultimately cool and then some
THE SHIT (adj.), top of the line
COLD-BLOODED (adj.), not nice
THE CRIB (n.), one's home, apartment, or room
THE BIG HOUSE (n.), prison
HOMIES (n.), one's group of friends
POSSE (n.), the group one spends time with
PEEPS (n.), one's people
GANGSTA (n.), an endearing expression for one who leads a dubious existence
G (n.), short for GANGSTA
40 (n.), a large can (generally 40 ounces) of beer
WORKS (n.), drugs
BUD (n.), marijuana
KILLER BUD (n.), better marijuana
K.G.B. (n.), killer green bud, even better marijuana
COINAGE (n.), money
411 (n.), information

DIGITS (n.), a phone number

MY BAD (n.), one's mistake

'HOOD (n.), the area of town in which one lives

OPP (n.), other people's property, someone else's girl-friend or boyfriend

JIMMY (n.), penis

JIMMY CAP (n.), condom

RACK (n.), a woman's breasts

BOOTIE (n.), a woman's behind

SLAMMIN' BOOTIE (n.), a very attractive woman's behind

WORD (v.), to listen carefully

WORD UP (v.), to listen even more carefully

WHAT'S UP G? (interj.), saying hello to a friend

HEY YO BO (interj.), saying hello to a friend

SHOUT OUT (interj.), another way of saying hello

PEACE OUT (interj.), saying good-bye

5000 (interj.), derived from the Audi 5000, derived from the old expression "out of here," shortened to "Audi," and finally, just "5000." In other words, another way of saying good-bye

BUST OUT (v.), to leave

BUST A MOVE (v.), to leave

KICKIN' IT (v.), to relax

CHILLIN' (v.), to relax

COOLIN' (v.), to relax

DIS (v.), to disrespect

FRONTIN' (v.), to disrespect with insult

WORD TO YOUR MOTHER (interj.), used to be "your mother," the worst possible insult

RECOGNIZE (v.), to show respect

GIVIN' PROPS (v.), to show support

REPRESENTIN' (v.), to speak for one's people

DOWN WITH THAT (v.), to agree

FREAKIN' (v.), to slightly lose control

PULL AN O.J. (v.), to completely lose control

INSANE IN THE MEMBRANE (adj.), out of one's mind

BUMP UGLIES (v.), to engage in sexual intercourse

HIP TO THE VIBE (adj.), to have an understanding of what the other person is going through

ON MY JOCK (adj.), a male expression to imply that a particular woman is sexually interested in him

KICK HIM/HER TO THE CURB (v.), to end a relationship

IN THE HOUSE (adj.), someone has arrived

KICKIN' AT THE CRIB (v.), relaxing at home

MAXIN' AND RELAXIN' (v.), to have fun and take it easy

TALKIN' SMACK (v.), to speak on a subject one knows little or nothing about

KNOW WHAT I'M SAYIN'? (or the abbreviated Know'm Sayin'?) (interj.), actual meaning, "You understand me," but it has become the way to end a sentence

EXERCISE

Translate the following paragraph into gangsta speak on the lines provided below.

I was spending some time with my group of friends, relaxing and taking it easy at home. After having a couple of beers, we decided to leave and take a walk around the block. On the way, we ran into another group of people, one of whom was with a very attractive girl whom my friend had recently broken up with. The two of them exchanged words, and my pal began to lose control slightly. The rest of us had to show support. After the other guy highly insulted my friend, we decided to continue on since they were speaking on a subject they knew nothing about.

_____

_____

_____

_____

_____

_____

If you translated this, you've just written your first rap song.

Surfers

The surfer lingo isn't as complex as gangsta lingo, simply because a great part of the day is spent lying, sitting, or standing on a surfboard. Anyway, the only thing that really needs to be communicated is who's got the next wave.

In light of that, you may still want to be able to have a conversation with them when you're at the beach because, after all, they are cute and have swimmers' bodies.

SURFER LEXICON

DUDE (n.), universal surfer word; replaces everyone's name. Also the way to begin and end every sentence

BRAU (n.), originates from the Hawaiian word *bruddeh*, which means "brother"

BRO (n.), Malibu slang for the above

RAD (adj.), short for radical; used to describe anything outstanding

THE KIND or DA KINE (adj.), the best

SICK (adj.), term for a great surfing maneuver or any other ridiculously dangerous stunt

RICHTER (v.), to ride the wave well

TEARING IT UP (v.), to ride the wave well

SHREDDING (v.), to maneuver the wave well

EPIC (adj.), the ultimate in something

LATE (adv.), derived from *later*

LATER (adv.), derived from *see you later*

WHAT UP (interj.), what's going on

BETTY (n.), a girl (a surf groupie)

BARNEY (n.), a goofy guy

HOTTY (n.), a cute guy or girl

FINEY (n.), a cute girl

NECTAR (n.), a really cute girl

CAKE (n.), money

REEFER (n.), marijuana

BREWSKY (n.), beer

SET (n.), a succession of good waves

EMOTIONAL GANGLIA (n.), a disorder that occurs after having a bad set

MELTDOWN (n.), when a person is very distraught

TUBE (n.), the hollow of a wave break

EXERCISE

Translate the following paragraph into surfer slang on the lines provided below.

My brother, what have you been doing? My friend, I had a monumental day whilst riding a succession of waves. I was terrific when I stayed on my surfboard in the hollow of the break. I did well. Really well. It defied sanity. Would you like to join me in a couple of beers? My girlfriend will pay. Great. We'll see you later, then.

_____

_____

_____

_____

_____

Translates to: Brau, what up? Dude, my set was epic. I got richter in the tube. Tearing it up, totally shredding. It was sick. Wanna have some brewskies? My Betty's got cake. All right. Late.

Trendoids

TRENDOID LEXICON

AS IF (adj.), highly unlikely
OH MY GOD (interj.), a prefix
TOTALLY (adv.), absolutely
WHATEVER (adv.), could care less
CHOKED (v.), to freeze emotionally
BALLISTIC (adj.), extremely upset
SCOPING (v.), to physically scan another person
LUMPED OUT (adj.), a car that is fully loaded
RETARD (n.), not bright
AIRHEAD (n.), not bright
VEGGING OUT (v.), to relax
MELLOWED (v.), to really relax

KILLER (adj.), great
STELLAR (adj.), really great
SOLID (v.), to confirm something
TOTALLY SPRUNG (adj.), completely infatuated
TOAST (adj.), burnt out
SNAGS (v.), to steal
SNAPS (v.), to give someone recognition
JEEPIN' (v.), to have sex (sometimes in a vehicle)
MONSTER (adj.), big, important
CHIN PUBES (n.), goatee
HEFFER (n.), an overweight person
HAUL ASS (v.), to hurry
SURFING THE CRIMSON TIDE (v.), to menstruate
SPARK UP (v.), to light a cigarette or a joint of marijuana
GET LACED (v.), to get stoned on a joint of marijuana
LOADIE (n.), someone who smokes marijuana
HEMP HUMPER (n.), someone who would do anything for marijuana, including engaging in sexual acts
CALORIE FEST (v.), to have a meal
HYMENALLY CHALLENGED (adj.), a virgin
STEMS (n.), legs
REEK (v.), to smell bad
RASHIN' (v.), to party
CLAM BAKE (n.), a party
PILE OF BRICKS (n.), one's house
HAGSVILLE (n.), a group of unattractive people
A FIN (n.), a five-dollar bill
BRUTALLY HOT (adj.), unbelievably good-looking
LIGHT IN THE LOAFERS (adj.), a homosexual male
DISCO-DANCIN' (adj.), a homosexual male
SUGAR IN THE BOOTS (adj.), to be a homosexual male

(continued on p. 108)

EXERCISE

Translate the following paragraph into trendoid slang on the lines provided below.

Hello. The party at Judy's parents' house last night really stunk of not very attractive people. After a quick look around the room, it was confirmed that every not bright guy with a goatee and every stupid girl discussing her period were just relaxing and smoking marijuana. The only people missing were homosexual men doing the hair and makeup of the girls that would look good only from far away. It made me very upset to the point of not caring.

_____

_____

_____

_____

_____

_____

_____

_____

_____

Translates to: Oh my God. Judy's clam bake at her parents' pile of bricks reeked of a trip to Hagsville last night. A quick scoping turned up solid that every retard with chin pubes and airhead crimson tide surfer were vegging out and sparking up. The only thing missing was a group of Streisand ticket holders doing the hair of these group of Monets. It left me ballistic. Whatever.

STREISAND TICKET HOLDER (n.), a homosexual
    male
CARPET MUNCHER (n.), a homosexual female
WAY HARSH (adj.), really mean
COMPLAINT ROCK (n.), alternative music
A BALDWIN (n.), a really cute guy
SHAME SPIRAL (v.), to feel guilty
MONET (n.), someone who looks good from afar but
    messy close up
TOOTHACHE (n.), someone who is too sweet

The Movie Industry

THE MOVIE INDUSTRY LEXICON

THE BUSINESS (n.), the only real business in the
    world, according to those in it
PLAYER (n.), someone important in the industry
POWER PLAYER (n.), a major film executive or movie
    star
STUDIO (n.), the mecca of Hollywood
COMER (n.), anyone on the rise
SEXY (adj.), someone or something that has appeal
HOT FOR IT (adj.), excited about anything
COVERAGE (n.), a job that requires the services of a
    bitter nonworking writer who reads a script, and
    usually passes on it, for $35 a script
TO PITCH, OR MAKE A PITCH (v.), to have an idea
    for a script, then beg a studio executive to make
    it a reality; if it happens, it usually takes about 10
    minutes
TAKE A MEETING (v.), when an executive has agreed

to listen to a pitch. Allotted time (in the exec's book): about six minutes, including greeting, coffee, and good-byes

ON CONFERENCE CALL (adj.), an assistant's polite way of telling a caller that he or she is not important to the assistant's boss, the executive

IN A MEETING (adj.), an assistant's polite way of telling a caller that he or she is not important to the assistant's boss, the executive

IN A CONFERENCE (adj.), an assistant's polite way of telling a caller that he or she is not important to the assistant's boss, the executive

I'LL PUT YOU ON THE CALL SHEET (interj.), an assistant's polite way of telling a caller that he or she is not important to the assistant's boss, the executive

OWES YOU A CALL (interj.), an executive's polite way of telling someone he or she is not important

AVAILABILITY (n.), work schedule of an actor or actress; with enough money on the table you can book them, even if they're dead or working straight for the next 10 years

WINDOW (n.), opening in schedule as determined by availability of talent (this includes being fired due to drug testing or any other form of lewd behavior on set)

GREEN LIGHT A PICTURE (v.), to give the go-ahead to move forward with the project

TURNAROUND (n.), your project has lost funding and therefore is now being passed around like an old hooker

HAVE A RELATIONSHIP (v.), a lie told to further oneself by claiming familiarity with powerful and famous people

IN BED WITH (v.), another lie told to further oneself; usually is literal

BIDDING WAR (n.), when you've convinced everyone that your script is the next *Schindler's List*

DEAL BREAKER (n.), can be anything from Sandra Bullock pulling out to an executive's drunk wife at a party

DEAL MAKER (n.), can be anything from Sandra Bullock putting out to an executive's drunk wife at a party

STAR VEHICLE (n.), any project that makes a star look good and gives him or her all the lines

HIGH CONCEPT (n.), usually a combination of stuff pulled from the newspaper and from action movies that we've all seen before

HOME RUN (n.), a hit movie

SELLING OUT (n.), any movie with Sandra Bullock

SCREENING (n.), a means of saving $8.50 on a bad movie, sans popcorn

INDEPENDENT (n.), used to be a low-budget art movie; now it's the only way to get an Academy Award nomination

Sorry, no exercise for this section. That's because most of the people who use the above terminology have no sense of humor; therefore, there is no reason to try and be funny by giving you an exercise. If you really want to see the lingo in action, pick up the trades.

COFFEEHOUSE GIRL

Watched too many Jean Seaberg films while eating mushrooms with a brownie chaser

Tattoo—image of Karl Marx

Tobacco companies—the only thing she doesn't protest

Only thing she doesn't hate is rebelling

I HATE THE SYSTEM
I HATE NEWT
I HATE RUSH LIMBAUGH
I HATE PETE WILSON
I HATE AUTHORITY

Only recently found out they make longer shirts

Loved emblem because of the two things it represents—her car and hemp being legalized

Belly ring was a gift from Jack Kerouac's niece

Refuses to admit copying underwear gimmick off Marky Mark

Paint splotches applied herself

Shoes stolen off dead uncle at funeral

THE WALLS HAVE EARS: TEN CONVERSATIONS OVERHEARD AROUND TOWN

AT FRED SEGAL

1. Mother: "Lisa, it's too small. If you rip it, I'll have to pay for it." Daughter: "So?"

AT BAR MARMONT

2. (1:45 A.M.—Last call)
   Single guy: "I'll have six Absoluts and cranberry, and she'll have a Diet Coke." Bartender: "Whatever."

AT WILD OATS (EXPENSIVE HEALTH FOOD STORE)

3. Seven-year-old to Mom, a rich producer's wife: "Dad orders pizza with everything whenever you're not home." Mom: "Your father's a pig and he makes me sick."

ACROSS TOWN AT EREWHON (SAME TIME)

4. Rocker: "I'm so used to ordering Damiano's with everything on it." Girlfriend: "Wow, you're so strong. This must be a challenge for you. Oh, did you get my brother the all-access pass for the KISS reunion tonight?"

AT A LAEMMLE THEATER

5. Agent: "I missed this one at Sundance." Friend: "Did I ask?"

6. Guy: "Ileana's a friend of mine." Girl: "She's been with Marty for years."

7. First agent: "You missed the White Party in Palm Springs. It was incredible." Second agent: "Really? Well, I had to baby-sit for Warren and Annette. I'm like an uncle."

AT JERRY'S DELI (3:15 A.M.)
8. Two neurotic comedians are arguing over the best pickle. First comedian: "Stage Deli. New York." Second comedian: "No, Katz's. Downtown."

AT LE PETIT FOUR (LUNCHTIME)
9. Two hideous French executives are discussing a deal. First executive: "Well, DeNiro passed, and Duvall. His wife knows Pacino, but I'm feeling good with Travolta. Does anyone know Travolta?" Second executive: "Well, we have a yes from Mickey Rourke." From the next table: "Who doesn't?"

AT LE DOME (MIDNIGHT)
10. Two women are at the bar, talking about a twenty-nine-year-old producer who's drunk and sitting alone at a nearby table eating a steak. First woman: "He thought I was an actress he'd seen, and then he asked me if I wanted to decorate his house." Second woman: "Well, he does have a Porsche."

POLITICAL SCIENCE MAJOR

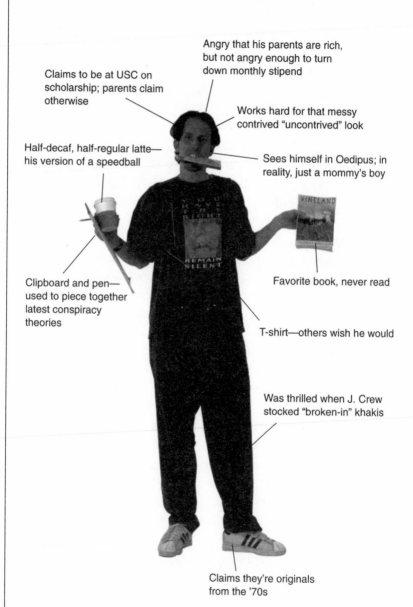

Angry that his parents are rich, but not angry enough to turn down monthly stipend

Claims to be at USC on scholarship; parents claim otherwise

Works hard for that messy contrived "uncontrived" look

Half-decaf, half-regular latte—his version of a speedball

Sees himself in Oedipus; in reality, just a mommy's boy

Clipboard and pen—used to piece together latest conspiracy theories

Favorite book, never read

T-shirt—others wish he would

Was thrilled when J. Crew stocked "broken-in" khakis

Claims they're originals from the '70s

AT 7:04 A.M.

1 Two agents are at breakfast. First agent: "If they think they're getting Streep, they're crazy. I actually know her, and her down time isn't until February." Second agent: "I know. I agree with you."

AT 9:15 A.M.

2 First woman: "My trainer said I had good genes." Second woman: "Yeah, that's great. Was that guy at Jerry's last night Persian or Italian?"

AT 10:30 A.M.

3 Single guy: "I'll have a croissant and a coffee, cream please. You're new, right, I've never met you, right?" Waitress: "I guess."

AT 1 P.M.

4 An actress is having lunch with her visiting sister. Actress: "My alterations will be ready at four, then he'll pick us up at seven for the screening. You should borrow something of mine." Sister: "Did your friend get the tickets for the Universal tour? I really don't want to miss it."

AT 4 P.M.

5 Same single guy from 10:30 A.M. (to-go cup in hand): "Do you know about the refills? I mean, being new and all?" Same waitress: "Yes."

AT 6 P.M.

6 Trainer: "I mean, I told her she had good jeans, but I meant her Levi's, not her thighs." Trainer's buddy: "Yeah. Is your brother still thinking about selling his Trans Am?"

AT 7 P.M.

7 Producer: "You know, since Ovitz left, it's just all different." Producer's eight-year-old child: "Shit happens."

AT 9 P.M.

8 Two actors are dining with their dogs after acting class. First actor: "It's funny—I'm okay with caffeine at night. I mean, if it keeps me up, I keep rehearsing my monologue. I feel good about it. Did you like what I did tonight in class?" Second actor: "What?"

AT 10:30 P.M.

9 Two people are talking after an AA meeting. First person: "It's just that I know it's the one-day-at-a-time thing, but when will he call?" Second person: "Did you see the speaker looking at me? I think he's cute. Does he have more than a year?"

10 Same single guy from 10:30 A.M. and 4 P.M.: "I
walked off with the cup, and I wanted to bring it
back to you so you didn't think I stole it."
Mexican busboy: *"Que?"*

10 WAYS TO HAVE A RELATIONSHIP IN HOLLYWOOD

1 Leave.

2 Become a dominatrix.

3 Pretend that the bald head, big nose, horrible table manners, and constant phone calls to Mother don't bother you.

4 Consult the Magic Eight-Ball.

5 Act like you don't want one.

6 Never return phone calls.

7 Always let them be right.

8 Go out of town a lot.

9 Be a really rich, famous, beautiful celebrity.

10 Be really cute and stupid.

10 WAYS NOT TO HAVE A RELATIONSHIP IN HOLLYWOOD

1 Be really smart, loving, independent, and attentive.

2 Share your thoughts.

3 Call.

4 Care.

5 Have sex with them.

6 Enjoy having sex with them.

7 Tell them you enjoy having sex with them.

8 Have a baby.

9 Have a better career than them.

10 Make the fatal mistake of saying, "I could really love you."

TOP 10 SIGNS THAT YOU'RE NOT MAKING ANY PROGRESS

1 You start to miss the country (even camping in bad weather sounds good again).

2 Your identity is as someone's girlfriend or boyfriend.

3 Your hair upkeep is higher than your rent.

4 You have a bus pass.

5 You look in the mirror and realize you're a poor man's Courtney Love.

6 You hope to be laid off so you can collect unemployment—it's better money.

7 You've started to send things home to your family to convince them you're doing well: i.e., photos of you with famous people (superimposed, of course).

8 The only doorman you know works at the Coconut Teaszer, and the only reason you know him is because he lives in your apartment building.

9 That little mole on your hand is starting to spread.

10 You thought you were broke, but you still manage to support your boyfriend.

TOP 10

SIGNS THAT YOU'RE MAKING SOME PROGRESS (BUT NOT MUCH)

1 You're dating Jerry Seinfeld's stand-in.

2 You're a guest on a talk show and the topic is "Dating Stand-Ins."

3 You bid and won a walk-on on "General Hospital" at a charity auction.

4 You don't have to wait in line at a club because the doorman recognizes you from a wet T-shirt contest.

5 You're getting a great tan driving around in your 1985 Chrysler LeBaron.

6 You're SAG-eligible.

7 Someone mistook you for Jennifer Aniston— obviously, that new cut is working for you.

8 You were invited to the wrap party for *Halloween 15*, and after some hesitation, they finally let you in.

9 Someone offered you money for sex, and this time you turned the person down.

10 The manager of your dry cleaners has asked for your head shot.

DO'S AND DON'TS ON GETTING YOUR SAG CARD

DO

1. Only sleep your way to a card if they're really cute (everyone will understand).

2. Go out with an unattractive casting director.

3. Do a nude scene in a show at the Coast Playhouse. Every agent in town will come. Someone will be attracted to you.

4. Go out with Oliver Stone.

5. Sleep with Steven Spielberg if you can.

DON'T

1. Pay a fee to a store that promises you both a SAG card and discount hair replacement.

2. Sleep with a producer under thirty.

3. Believe an actor can help you.

4. Hang around the set, hoping for a line, because the key grip told you he could hook you up (we know what he really wants).

5. Believe the nude scene you've just finished is going into a SAG-accredited movie.

TOP 10 MOST UNBELIEVABLE TRUTHS ABOUT HOLLYWOOD

1 It exists.

2 It actually gets some good movies made (somehow, and not many).

3 Sometimes it rains.

4 Number-one language of Beverly Hills: Farsi.

5 People don't always tell the truth (surprise!).

6 People drive to their next-door neighbor's house (really).

7 Sometimes you meet smart people (sometimes).

8 Sometimes you meet nice people (sometimes).

9 People actually live in the Valley.

10 The nose you meet may not be the original.

TOP 10 CELEBRITY KILLERS (CONVICTED OR NOT)

1 O.J. Simpson (victims: Ron Goldman and Nicole Brown and daytime TV)

2 Erik and Lyle Menendez (victims: dominating parents)

3 Don Simpson (victim: Don Simpson)

4 Fatty Arbuckle (victim: some drunken starlet)

5 Charles Manson (victims: Sharon Tate, Linda Folger, etc., and the career of the actor who portrayed him in the TV movie)

6 Charles Rathbun (victim: Lynda Sobek, and the modeling test shoot)

7 Michael Cimino (victim: MGM)

8 Renny Harlin (victim: Geena Davis's career)

9 William Randolph Hearst (victim: Orson Welles's career)

10 Hollywood itself (victims: too numerous to mention)

EVERYTHING ELSE

Oh, right. We forgot to tell you. Some other things you might want to know about Hollywood and its environs. These include unpredictable, uncontrollable acts of nature and volatile rage. That is, earthquakes, mudslides, floods, fires, riots, gangs, the LAPD, overprocessed hair, traffic jams, smog, the Valley, Silver Lake, former police chief Daryl Gates, Governor Pete Wilson, muggings at ATM machines, the DMV, bad tap water, medflies, overpopulation, Rodney King, skin cancer.

There you have it. If you can make it through all of that, you're a survivor. You've got what it takes. Isn't it fantastic? Nobody back home could live through a week of this, and you wear it like a badge of honor. It's

a proud way of life. It's like being part of one huge dysfunctional family. But let's face it. The whole world wants to be like us, because we're all so much more fun than the rest. Kids in Japan follow our every trend. We are worshiped universally. So hold your head up high and soak in those UV rays. YOU'VE MADE IT! YOU'RE A HOLLYWOOD-ITE!

P.S. If the above doesn't apply to you, and you find yourself longing for anything that feels like substance, and suddenly your boring life back in that small town seems like a long-lost dream, then run, run, run! Make that plane! We hope you get an extra bag of peanuts. Like most of those who come here only to flee, once you're home, the closest you'll ever want to be to this town again is at your local movie theater. So enjoy the quiet life. You won't be missed. Bye bye.

PHOTO ACKNOWLEDGMENTS

HOLLYWOOD WANNA-BE:	Kevin Dornan
WESTSIDE TRENDY GIRL:	Dianna Miranda
RRRRIOT GRRRRL:	Quiet
OUT-OF-WORK ACTOR GUY:	Eddie McClintock
DOG:	Rupy
MODEL/ACTRESS/WHATEVER (MAW):	Shari Bedard
HOLLYWOOD AGENT:	Rick Penn-Kraus
PUBLICIST:	Emily Wagner
THE ASSISTANT:	Alex Manette
ROCKER AND GIRLFRIEND PROP:	Steve Olsen, Robin Greer
THE SUNDANCE MAN:	Peter Feldman
GANGSTA:	Kwame James
COFFEEHOUSE GIRL:	Sarah Reinhardt
POLITICAL SCIENCE MAJOR:	Bodhi Elfman